D0341366

Online Marketing

Online Marketing

A User's Manual

Murray Newlands

WILEY

A John Wiley and Sons, Ltd, Publication

ISBN 978-0-470-97384-4 (hardback), ISBN 978-1-119-97453-6 (ebook)

ISBN 978-1-119-99277-6 (ebook), ISBN 978-1-119-99278-3 (ebook)

A catalogue record for this book is available from the British Library.

Set in 11/16pt Adobe Jenson Pro by Sparks – www.sparkspublishing.com
Printed in Great Britain by TJ International Ltd, Padstow, Cornwall

*To my parents, George and Elizabeth,
as well as my brothers Stewart and Craig*

Contents

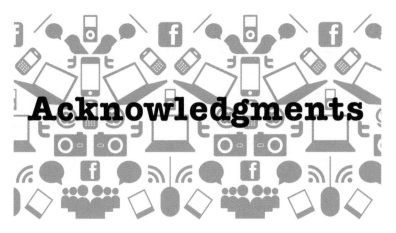

Acknowledgments

I hope this book will serve as an inspiration to all bloggers seeking a book deal. This book came about through my editor Ellen Hallsworth approaching me to write for John Wiley having read my blog www.murraynewlands.com. It can happen! I would like to thank Ellen who has become a friend during this book for all her suggestions and hard work in helping this project succeed.

I am indebted both consciously and unconsciously to a great many people for their help, support and inspiration when I needed it. Two bloggers who inspired me right from the start are Heather Smith, HeatherinBC.com and Steve Hall, Adrants.com. Chris Brogan reached out to me as I was just starting and has encouraged me along my journey. I'd like to express my gratitude to my business partner in Influence People, Luke Brynley-Jones, for the global trip we have been on.

I would also like to thank in no particular order Sue Keogh, Pierre Zarokian, Andrew Bennett, Dana Oshiro, Holly Homer, Chris Tew, Nadeem Azam, Warren Whitlock, Jonathan Volk, Jennifer Lindsay, Tom Foremski, Oliver Roup, Kristi Hines, Dazzlin Donna Fontenot, Connie Roberts, Ann Smarty, Gail Gardner, Ron Cripps, John Chow, Tamara Walker, Scott James, Vandy Massey, Nick Welsh, Geoff Jones, Filip Matous, Shawn Collins, Missy Ward, Emma Jones, Eric

Schechter, Marissa Louie, Greg Rollett, Jorgen Sundberg, Katja Garrood, James Evans and Brian Solis – and my dad for casting a professorial eye over the draft.

Murray Newlands,
Cambridge, New York and San Francisco

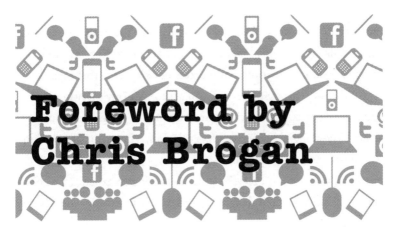

Foreword by Chris Brogan

Near as I can recall, I met Murray Newlands because I really liked his shirt. It was a nice shirt, with all sorts of embroidery bits on it, and very, very white. Murray stood out in a crowd, and when I went to say hello, he was very polite and personable. It's in these simple ways that first impressions are made.

And now, here I am writing a foreword for Murray's new book. I'm fairly late in handing it in, because like all Internet marketer types, I've got three thousand projects on the go, and like all professional speakers, I'm up the night before a trip, trying to work through some more of my to-do list instead of sleeping soundly, and like all entrepreneurs, this is the night before the launch of my new project, Kitchen Table Companies.

What goes into a foreword? Well, in most cases, you're hoping that I'll help you decide that this book is totally worth it. In some cases (fewer), you're just a nerd who reads EVERY WORD IN A BOOK (I'm that kind of nerd sometimes). In a middling number of cases, you're someone who knows me and wonders what I'm doing endorsing Murray Newlands in this way.

Murray's book is worth a read because it goes fairly deeply into all the current best and known trends and practices for doing Internet marketing. He covers all the social media stuff that's all the rage, but Murray also covers email marketing, affiliate marketing, and all kinds of other great information that sets this book apart in that regard.

All the way through, the 'feel' you get for Murray's writing is what you'd get if you spoke with him for more than two minutes. Murray is a very easy-going, down-to-earth gentleman, who seems like the kind who'd patiently hold your hand and help you through the foggy parts until you understood everything he was trying to explain. The book reads that way, which is delightful, because that's exactly who Murray is in person.

This book is actionable. It's useful. It's the kind of book that you'll keep in an easy-to-reach area. If you're the kind of person who wants to understand what's what before diving in, Murray's given you all you need to get started. If you buy another book to read after this one, you're kind of stalling, and you should rethink that move. At least in the short term. Take a look at what you've got here and execute from this playbook for a while, okay?

Finally, because it's not like they asked me to write Murray's book for him, I wanted to say that picking up a book like this one is actually the start of something exciting. Get a note pad. Crack open a web browser. And get thinking about how you're going to execute these things. Because that's the bigger opportunity with a book like this. You can do something big with it right away.

Are you ready? Let's let Murray do his thing.

    – Chris Brogan, President & CEO, Human Business Works

    www.humanbusinessworks.com

Introduction

Everything You Want to Know but are Afraid to Ask about a New Kind of Marketing

A friend of mine, we'll call him Tim, has been a marketing professional for decades. He's been successful, consistent and innovative. A few months ago his boss called him in and said, "We need to get on top of our digital strategy. I want to revamp our website and start a blog, get some SEO going and make sure we are doing everything we can with social media and affiliate marketing."

Tim said sure thing, tried not to sweat, and immediately went to his desk and called me.

"Murray, I don't really know what digital strategy is, I've barely heard of blogs and social media and I have no idea what SEO even stands for. Help!"

We spent a lot of time talking on the phone over the next few weeks, and he put together a digital marketing strategy that worked and made his boss happy. But for everyone like Tim who has someone like me to call there are a thousand others who have nowhere to turn.

This book is for you.

It will explain the basics, teach you techniques and strategies, and connect you with the best resources out there. This book will show you how to plan, execute, manage and measure a successful online marketing campaign.

THE MARKETING WORLD

In less than ten years the entire landscape of marketing has changed. What a few years ago was a new option is quickly becoming the new way of doing things. Not making the transition could mean losing your job or your company's place in the market.

A successful marketing professional in 1999 knew how to put together a direct mail campaign with a dynamic copywriter and targeted mailing lists, delivering a 3% conversion rate. Maybe their daughter was using an email account at college.

By 2004, that same marketer needed to turn their direct mail into an email campaign, build a landing page that converted leads and figure out a reliable way for their customers to buy something online. Facebook's founder was still in high school.

Fast forward to now. There are over 500 million people on Facebook and over 50 million "tweets" happening every day. Online marketing has exploded, leaving many traditional marketing techniques gathering dust in the corner with carbon copy machines or in the storage room with lead paint.

Do you know how to coordinate a website, online PR and an affiliate marketing campaign to reach potential customers? Do you know how to use digital branding, SEO and social media to make sure your business is dynamic and easy to find?

If you need to start from scratch, this book will help you. If you already know some of the pieces and just want to round out your understanding of all the options out there, this book will help you.

WHAT WILL THIS BOOK TEACH?

This book is ideal to use both as an introduction that you can read straight through and as a reference to keep on your shelf and come back to when you need it. I'll be covering all aspects of online marketing – company websites, social media, digital branding, blogging, video, search engine optimization (SEO), email marketing, affiliate marketing, online PR, and digital advertising.

This book will help you:

- understand the basics across the spectrum of online marketing,
- develop online marketing skills that you can use today,
- deliver scalable results,
- monitor and measure your campaign, and
- grow your business.

Here's a preview of what's in store.

CHAPTER 1 – SOCIAL MEDIA

Social media is the darling topic of the moment that your boss tells you "you have to do." The computer company Dell makes millions from it every year, but how can *you* use social media to generate traffic, leads and sales for your company? I will go into Twitter, Facebook, Google and other emerging social media tools that offer endless possibilities.

CHAPTER 2 – DIGITAL BRANDING

Companies are developing more personality-focused brands because consumers relate better to people and characters than corporate entities. At the same time, personal branding is growing in importance as a business asset. Brand reputation management is just as important as what you say on your website – maybe more.

CHAPTER 3 – COMPANY WEBSITES

With a growing proportion of business happening online, your company's website is critical. Company websites are far more than just putting your brochure online. Your customers expect news, real-time feeds, video and newsletter subscriptions with the site as the hub of activity that extends to social media like Facebook and Twitter.

CHAPTER 4 – BLOGGING

Blogs give everyone the ability to publish, and blogging for business offers an incredible opportunity to get news out to your current and potential customers. But they also raise a number of questions. Who should write it? What should you say? How do you manage employee disclosures?

CHAPTER 5 – ONLINE PR AND BLOGGER OUTREACH

Online PR is predicted to be one of the fastest growing sectors of the online marketing industry. Social media is heavily intertwined with content creation and written content is still a very large part of this. Traditional PR skills will need to be refocused in order for new horizons to appear. Online PR is now heavily intertwined with SEO, with some SEO firms offering PR and PR firms offering SEO services.

CHAPTER 6 – VIDEO MARKETING

Video is one of the easiest ways to make a personal connection with your audience. From corporate videos to funny viral videos, YouTube's success demonstrates the potential to reach large numbers with online video. The process of utilizing video for business can be a lot easier and a lot less expensive than you think.

CHAPTER 7 – SEO

SEO stands for Search Engine Optimization. Being found online by your current and future customers is vital to success. Knowing the basics is a must so that you can implement campaigns the right way and understand how to find and manage external agencies.

CHAPTER 8 – EMAIL MARKETING

Email marketing is more than just redesigning print mailers online, it is about developing a new relationship with customers. The transition from direct postal mail to email has been one that many marketers are familiar with, and the next phase in the evolution of this medium is the integration with social media campaigns. Add to that options like Facebook Connect, Twittering and Share-ability buttons to content and you can dramatically increase reach and grow email lists.

CHAPTER 9 – AFFILIATE MARKETING

Affiliate marketing used to be a specialist's art form – now it is much more mainstream, encompassing business-to-business products and services as well as consumer needs. Preparing a company for affiliate marketing, selecting an affiliate network and recruiting affiliates can seem like a daunting task to those unfamiliar with the territory; however, the rewards can be significant.

CHAPTER 10 – DIGITAL ADVERTISING

Advertising has not gone away – it has changed. Millions of pounds are spent on pay-per-click advertising and Google very quickly introduced image banners to its advertising inventory. Ad banners now include data collection forms and additional features that make them much more effective.

WHAT YOU GET

Each chapter is structured upon similar lines and covers the following key areas.

- Introduction
- The Basics
- How to Use it in Practice
- Examples
- Advanced Uses
- What the Future Holds
- Tools and Resources

You won't become an "expert" overnight, but (to answer a question I get a lot) no one's an expert – yet. The rapid growth of an entirely new kind of marketing is both exciting and frightening, and everyone has a lot to learn.

This is a resource guide for the million questions you have to ask but can't – because if you're in marketing, *you are* the person that everyone you know is asking.

Keep asking questions, and start reading for the answers.

Chapter 1

Social Media – Facebook, Twitter, LinkedIn

INTRODUCTION

Social media is about creating conversations and cultivating relationships online. As a marketer, you need to understand that it's already mainstream, not something in the distant future. Twitter sees more than 50 million status updates every day – larger than the population of England – and Facebook has over 500 million registered profiles – that's larger than the population of the United States. And while there is a lot to learn about social media, at its core it is just what it says it is – social. You will hear a lot of buzz terms like "Listening" or "Viral" or "Engage," and these are all important tactics within social media marketing, but, as I said, the key thing to remember is that all social media is about communication and relationships.

So what does social media mean for marketing? Marketing in the 20th century was primarily about broadcasting a message and interrupting what people were doing to tell them your message. In the 21st century social media marketing is about engaging in relationships with your customers and making your message and brand part of their online experience.

People online are embracing brands through social media:

- 46% of Facebook users say they would talk about or recommend a product on Facebook.
- 44% of Twitter users have recommended a product.
- 25% of search results for the World's Top 20 largest brands are links to user-generated content.
- 73% of active online users have read a blog.
- 34% of bloggers post opinions about products and brands.

And the number that tells the whole story of the transition from 20th century interruption-based marketing to 21st century social media relationship-based marketing?

- 78% of consumers trust peer recommendations. Only 14% trust advertisements.

People are not just using social media, they trust it. Chris Brogan and Julien Smith wrote an entire book called *Trust Agents* about how to operate as part of that give and take, how to use the web to build influence, improve reputation and earn trust.

Where things like billboards interrupted your drive, commercials interrupted your TV show, or magazine ads interrupted the article you were reading, social media is the opposite. Instead of interrupting, social media marketing is about making your message part of the media a customer or potential customer is consuming, enjoying, or taking part in.

Social media marketing is about becoming part of the user experience for your customers, both current and potential. You are not becoming something that adorns the side of the page, you are not becoming something that will interrupt the user experience, you are not becoming something that people click away from as soon as they realize it is there. Leave that to the Internet advertising world. Social media marketing does not interrupt – it integrates.

Whenever I talk about the process, people always ask me when they start to make money out of it – where's the ROI? How will I know if it's working? Even though people know that social media is happening all around them, there still aren't hard and fast rules about what "success" means. And that's both the beauty of and the problem with social media marketing – there is no formula. The way to think about success is to figure out your goals – whether those be building account size, creating engagement, or selling products – and establish your own targets for "success."

 THE BASICS

Social media marketing is about becoming part of a community and integrating your messaging with the larger context of that community. In this chapter I will discuss how to assess, establish, utilize and monitor your company's social media presence. Then I'll look more specifically at how to create a presence or campaign on larger social media networks like Twitter, Facebook, YouTube and LinkedIn.

YOUR SOCIAL MEDIA PRESENCE

Steps to creating your social media presence

1 Assess your current social media presence.
2 Research potential social media networks to join.
3 Adapt your existing content to your chosen networks.
4 Strategically plan your overall social media campaign.
5 Craft your social media presence.
6 Create new content for social media.
7 Listen to your potential customers where they already are.
8 Engage with your customers.
9 Represent your product/service as part of the brand.
10 Measure your influence and tweak your approach.

1   Assess your current social media presence

Before you can figure out where you want to go with your social media marketing, you have to know where you are, so first things first: where are you? Most people I know say something like, "Well, I started a Twitter account a while back but I haven't used it, and I don't even remember the password," or "I have a Facebook page but it's been a while since I was there." If that sounds like you, the first thing to do is stop worrying about it.

Make a list of the social media networks you are active in. And if you can dig up those old passwords through the clunky retrieval processes, it's worth the ten minutes. Take some time to go back through the accounts and see what you posted, think about what you were trying to do, and how it felt to be on social media at all. Whether you stopped a while back, keep up with one or more accounts, or haven't started at all, be honest with yourself about why – that is the first question to address.

2   Research potential social media networks to join

There are hundreds of different social media networks and sites that you can join. That doesn't mean that you need to join all of them. What it means is you have a lot of choices to make.

The vast majority of the social media networks out there are geared toward niche audiences, or have become that way over time. For example, Sphinn.com is a social media network specifically for Internet marketing professionals. It's designed for industry people to share articles, hold discussions, find events and network. If you're looking for celebrity gossip or a new band, it's not here. It will never be huge because it's a niche market. But if you are looking for a way to connect with and learn from other Internet marketers, it's ideal. The lower number of people is an advantage, rather than trying to hunt down the Internet marketers on LinkedIn or Facebook.

On the other hand, MySpace used to be the go-to personal social network. They lost that market for a variety of reasons, but they temporarily re-emerged as a destination for musicians and artists. This is where you find that new band, but not where you go to talk about search engine optimization.

Depending on who you want to reach, you'll want to research the best social media networks for your niche. Wikipedia (www. en.wikipedia.org/wiki/List_of_social_networking_websites) has a good list to start with, and Googling your niche market with + social media will give you some options as well.

That said, I do recommend establishing accounts on Twitter, Facebook and LinkedIn and keeping them updated. Setting aside time each day to check each one is ideal, but checking each one once per week is the minimum. Remember, social media is intended to be real-time, i.e. a form of simultaneous communication, and it's social too.

3   Adapt your existing content to your chosen networks

Before you open new accounts, you need to get some content ready. While you may hear the mantra that "content is king," it's a little misleading. Having content ready and creating a schedule for its release is the ideal way to make sure you have something to contribute once you join the social media networks of your choosing. When you are researching those networks, get a sense of what other people are sharing. Look at your partners and competitors – how are they using social media? Links? White papers? Videos? The culture of what to share is most likely already established and will give you a good starting point for deciding what of your own content is ideal to share on other networks.

When you are deciding what to share and when, keep in mind that you can adapt some of your content. If you have a great PowerPoint about sailing and you want to share it on YouTube, consider presenting it to your company as a speech and putting it on video. Or adapting it to a few key statistics or statements on each page and adding music. You get the idea.

4   Cultivate your social media presence

Start by watching and listening to what is going on in the networks already. Spend a week or two just seeing what the culture is like and if you want to be part of the conversation. This will look different depending on the network, but making connections, engaging in interactions and promoting the content of other people in the network is an ideal place to start. Build the community first, then look at how your content fits in the mix.

Then, when you decide where to engage, I recommend starting out with a set of goals based on interacting. For example, you could set a goal of making 50 connections, having at least 10 conversations and re-sharing 10 pieces of content within the network during your first week. And while you're at it, don't share any of your own content.

No matter what your field, seek out current experts in the space, current customers, and current discussions or posts about your industry. What are people saying? What are the problems that they are having? What frustrations do you see?

From there, decide what problem your product or service solves and make that your role on the network. This will give you an angle for conversations, a connecting thread throughout the content you share and, eventually, a reason for people to seek you out.

Choosing something like "sailing" is much too general. You could end up sharing and talking about everything from the America's Cup to where to find the best repair shop on the coast. To craft a social media presence, take your personal or company mission statement and adapt it to the network you are on – it will give you direction, purpose and, with time, a branded presence that people will begin to recognize.

5　Strategically plan your overall social media campaign

Yes, you can open a few social media accounts, fish around and hope for the best, but I don't recommend it. Think about the last time you went to a networking event and thought, well, I'll just go in and see who's there. Did you end up hanging out at the buffet and having a drink? Forget your business cards?

Don't let your social media experience be like that. Like any other endeavor, you want to have goals and a plan to meet them.

Start with one or two goals on a given social media network. Know what you want to do and who you want to meet, and make sure the content you create and share addresses those goals.

6　Create new content for social media

Once you have spent a week or two focusing on listening, interacting and understanding how the community works, it's time to start creating new content that is tailored to solving problems, crafting your personal brand, or deepening the connections you've already started.

If you've found certain problems that your product or service solves, package them in a way that is easy to share and that makes sense for your network. If you have found things you like that other people are doing, tailor those techniques to your own account and approach. If you've made connections, figure out what would take that connection to the next step – whether that's converting a lead, creating a business partnership, or offering advice.

Does that sound like a lot of work? It is. And just a few minutes ago you didn't think you'd have much to say on a social networking website.

7   Listen to your potential customers where they already are

I could have put this earlier in the list, but I think it's important to focus on this after you have started to create content. It's an easy trap to listen at the beginning, then just start creating content and churning it out, turning your social media into a broadcast network. Remember to listen as you go – it's how you started, and it will always be a bottomless well of ideas and direction for what you need to make and where you need to go next.

8   Engage with your customers

Some of this is listening, some of this is creating content that solves problems or converts leads, but what I mean by "engage" is to interact. When you come into contact with current or potential customers, be yourself. Be human. One of the truly amazing (and often difficult) things about social media is that it allows and sometimes compels you to interact as a person, not just as a business. Embracing that can be hard, especially for marketing departments, but it goes back to one of the core principles about social media – it's social. Remember, you're talking *with* people, not *at* them.

9   Represent your product/service as part of the brand

The idea of branding in social media is important, and everyone has a different version of why, how to do it, and what a good "brand" is. In the end, your "brand" is the culture around what you represent, the feeling you or your customers have about it, and the sum total of what all those interactions say about you.

Realize that just because someone has bought your product or used your service and been happy with it does not mean he/she becomes an instant advocate. Treating all of your interactions as if those people are going to turn around and share their interaction with the rest of the network will keep you grounded – and a lot of times, those people will be sharing their sense and satisfaction level of your interaction. It's the double-edged sword that is social media.

10 Measure your influence and tweak your approach

I'll get into some specific monitoring service options later, and these will change depending on your campaign goals, but it's important to remember that you should monitor (from the beginning) and keep adjusting what you are doing based on what you find out. Social media requires a lot of adjustments along the way – it's like having a conversation – and there are social media monitoring solutions that range from free DIY versions to robust reporting structures. In the early stages you'll probably be doing a lot of adjusting, and that doesn't mean you're failing – it means you're learning.

 HOW TO USE IT IN PRACTICE: DEVELOPING YOUR SOCIAL MEDIA PRACTICE

There are four big social media networks that I believe everyone should be part of: Twitter, Facebook, LinkedIn, YouTube. In addition, there is a strong momentum building for geo-location, meaning that you can tie your social media interactions to a specific place. That area is building steam and has a variety of networks that I'll discuss at the end of the chapter.

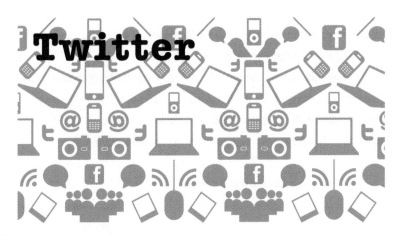

INTRODUCTION

Twitter was founded in 2007 by Jack Dorsey and Biz Stone. The problem they wanted to solve? They were looking for a way to share messages with everyone in the office at the same time that would work from their cell phones and was smoother than the clunky email list. They came up with Twitter and changed social media forever.

TWITTER BASICS

Twitter is simple to use and doesn't take long to set up. And it's user-friendly. Whereas many people find it hard to blog because they don't think of themselves as writers, Twitter actually limits you to use only 140 characters per post (originally due to SMS texting limits).

Twitter is often called "micro-blogging," which is essentially using short communication snippets to do what blogs do – relate or comment on news, present views and opinions, or communicate with customers, colleagues and new people. Twitter is made up of 50 million+ users, all of whom can say whatever they like and have the ability to listen to everyone else. The possibilities are incredible.

Twitter, like many things in life, has its own set of jargon and terminology. Unless you have used Twitter, it can seem baffling. The great thing is that the basic terminology is actually very limited. On Twitter, there are a few key terms to know when you're starting out:

- A "tweet" is a message you type into Twitter.
- To "follow" someone is to have their "tweets" published on your homepage. When you start, you follow people you know or want to know – that means anytime they tweet a message it shows up on your homepage stream. Once you start participating, other people will follow you and you'll have "followers," which means everything you tweet will show up on their homepage stream.

People love the immediacy of the content and the ability to get involved. Have you ever been at a party and wanted to be in every conversation at the same time? Twitter offers you that ability and you will not miss anything.

If you are planning to use Twitter I would suggest you first consider what you are going to use that profile for. Who are you going to communicate with, and what will they want to engage you with?

The trend towards personalized business and connecting on a personal level with a customer or influencer about both social issues and business is increasingly important. Some people want to use Twitter for personal reasons as well as business – this can present a problem, because often your customers don't want to know the same information as your friends do, and vice versa. But as an individual marketer or someone tweeting for your company, the sweet spot is finding the right balance of business-related content and personable touches.

Decide at the start what the purpose of your Twitter account will be. Is it work, personal, product- or service-oriented? Your bio information will be based on this purpose, as will the original sets of people you set out to follow.

@ ADVANTAGES OF TWITTER

I have used Twitter to build great relationships. I have seen traffic to my blog increase in quality and have received targeted traffic that has lead to business partnerships and sales within the first 20 days.

One good way to get an idea of Twitter is to follow some prominent Twitter users and just watch what they do. I recommend you follow me at www.twitter.com/murraynewlands and other prominent Twitter users and choose the parts of our approaches you wish to take.

Unless you are Stephen Fry I do not care if you are having coffee! Do you care if I am having coffee? No, I thought not … and you will unfollow me because you do not know me and don't care about the miniscule details of my life. Just because people hang on Stephen Fry's every "tweet" does not mean you or I can tweet like him. Think about what you are saying and to whom. Stephen Fry has an adoring fan base. You may have friends, colleagues, clients, business associates, your mom and your kids as your followers. I may be interested to know you are paying a visit to New York because I may be there. Others may not.

Another way of thinking about it is that you probably say things and talk in a different way to your mom than to your friends in a bar. Remember each audience is different.

TWITTER OVERVIEW

Think of Twitter as a communication channel where others can comment on what you say and you can comment on what they say – it's a conversation. Once you start to follow a few people and see what they are saying and they follow you back, it is very easy to join conversations. By all means say what you want to say but make sure it is interesting to those who are reading.

Twitter is not like Messenger with 140 characters, unless you are communicating to a very small group. You are communicating with the world at large even if at the moment there are only a few people reading your updates. What you say remains on the Internet as part of your Twitter account, so it is forever part of your brand.

You may want to select a small group of people to follow and get into conversation with before you venture too far, and have a public conversation with hundreds of people following you and those whom you are following.

Twitter may be confusing if you haven't used it, but after 10 minutes most people I know have worked it out. It's straightforward to understand and people I know have become very comfortable using Twitter in a short time.

But before you can start using it, you have to sign up.

 ## HOW TO GET STARTED USING TWITTER

- Step 1: Signing up. Go to Twitter and click on the "Get Started" button.
- Step 2: Follow the simple instructions to complete the process. Think carefully about what username you want to choose for

yourself – make sure it is something people will recognize and ideally something they would search for.

- Step 3: Add a picture. Choose a picture of you rather than a logo or picture of your product. People are much more likely to follow and interact with you if they are looking at the image of a real person, rather than a picture.
- Step 4: Add a URL. Under the "Account Information" tab you can add your URL. I added www.murraynewlands.com because this blog is the hub of my online activity. Set this to the page you think would be most relevant to Twitter users from this account. If that is your company, then direct followers to that website. If the website is very general you may want to think about a special landing page just for people coming from Twitter. Newcomers to your profile may well check out your website and if getting them to your website is one of your objectives, then this is a critical step.
- Step 5: Add a bio. People follow people they like and think are interesting. This is the place to sell yourself. You have 160 characters to make a good impression and persuade them that reading further and even following you and listening to what you say is going to be of interest to them. If your bio reads "I am going to sell you stuff," it is not going to attract many followers. If you just say "Hello," that does not tell the user anything about you. Have a look at what other people say in their bios before deciding what to put in yours. I recommend making it clear what you do and adding a few words that will make you stand out.
- Step 6: Choose your password. This should be six characters long and not a regular dictionary word.
- Step 7: Devices. This is for connecting Twitter to your mobile phone, which is what Twitter was created for initially. If you enter your cell phone number here you'll be able to text in messages to

your Twitter account. If you have a smartphone, there are numerous Twitter apps that are much better equipped to make using Twitter an easy and enjoyable process. You can have your Twitter messages sent to your mobile phone as texts. This is a great feature if you want to be updated while on the move. This can also get very expensive if you don't have an unlimited text or data plan, so I recommend using the email version for updates instead.

- Step 8: Notices. When you first get started you probably will want to receive all the notices and if you keep it to a small group of people you may want to keep the notices on. If you move beyond 500 followers you will probably want to turn the notices off. The more followers you have, the more followers you will get.

- Step 9: Your first post on Twitter. Posting on Twitter is very easy once you have an account. Go to the top of your homepage where you will see the question "What's Happening?" and post any message you like as long as it is only 140 characters long. Type your message in the box and then press update and it will be published to the world.

But before you start – STOP.

Think about your first post. What are you going to say? What impression do you want to give? Remember what you want to use this profile for. "What's Happening?" can mean so much to so many different people. If your boss/customer/supplier asked you, "What's Happening?" you would not say, "Getting coffee in Starbucks." You might say that to a friend. "What's Happening?" could mean launching a new project or planting a tree. What does it means in the context of the profile you are building?

ADVANCED FEATURES

@ REPLIES

Once you are following people and they tweet messages you will see their tweets appear on your Twitter page. If you want to reply to something they twittered you can press the reply arrow on the side of the post as it comes in or you can use the @ sign and then their user name.

To send me a message, type @murraynewlands. Then you type what you want to say to me and press tweet. This message is visible to me and everyone else following you. If the other person replies in the same way you will be having a public conversation in front of all your followers, and theirs. Your followers can then enter into conversation with you, and theirs with them. That is how conversations spread.

To reply to me you would type:

@murraynewlands Thank you for your book about Twitter.

If you click the @Replies link on the right hand side of your Twitter page you can see all the users who have replied to you.

DIRECT MESSAGES

You do not always want to send communications publicly for everyone who follows you on Twitter to read. You can send private messages directly to people who follow you. You can only send direct messages to people who are following you. The way to send a direct message is to type D then a space before the user name. To send me a direct message, I would need to be following you and then you would type:

D murraynewlands Thank you for your book about Marketing.

If you click the direct messages link on the right hand side of your Twitter page you can see all the users who have sent you direct messages. You will see a dropdown list of people to send direct messages to, but this is not the full list of people following you.

 TWITTER EXAMPLES

DELL: A CASE STUDY

@Dell is one of the most famous and profitable examples of using Twitter as a sales vehicle. There are real people keeping tabs on their Twitter stream, answering questions and seeking out conversations about computers. The people working the account are there to answer questions, follow leads, and make the experience of looking for a computer online as personable as going to a store. Dell attributes over $100 million in computer sales to their Twitter account.

@COMCASTCARES

One of the other most famous examples is @comcastcares. Comcast is one of the largest cable providers in the United States. Cable television is something people love to complain about, and Comcast noticed that people love to complain about it on Twitter. So they created a team at the address @comcastcares to address those concerns the same way a customer service telephone line would. They started solving problems and set the tone for Twitter to be used for just this purpose. And they have been rewarded with status as an industry leading user and lots of happy messages from those who were complaining.

ADVANCED USES OF TWITTER

- **#hashtags** allow you to denote a word or set of characters for a special purpose. They can be created by anyone and there is not a central registry of hashtags. These are particularly useful for groups or groupings and to enable terms to be searched. If I were planning a birthday party I would tweet "I am having a party on X at Y let me know if you can come #murrayp" Anyone wanting to see who else was coming would be able to search for "murrayp."

  This is typically used for conferences or topical discussions. For example, a Twitter conference may use #140tc so that it's easy to follow a conference-wide conversation. Alternately, marketing professionals may add #marketing to their tweets when they want them to be found in the larger, industry specific Twitter stream.

- **Lists.** Lists are a relatively new feature on Twitter. It allows anyone to take a group of Twitter users and put them all on a list. For example, I may want to take all of the affiliate marketing bloggers I read and put them on a list called "affiliates." Then anytime I want to see only what that group is tweeting about I can click on that link. In addition, if someone visits my Twitter page and they want to follow all of the affiliate bloggers that I follow, they can click on the link and follow the entire list. It's a powerful way to get to know the people you follow.

- **Free Twitter profile designer.** Use pre-made backgrounds or design your own to create and personalize your profile. There are lots of free Twitter profile design sites. Twitter often has challenges with uploading images so you may have to be a bit patient. If you really want a customized Twitter background, there are people who you can pay to design one.

THE FUTURE OF TWITTER

Twitter is expanding in several important ways.

1   **Real-time news source.** In addition to growing their user base, Twitter has changed its original purpose along the way. What was once seen as a way for groups of people to message each other soon morphed into a way for people who didn't know each other find and meet each other. Then it became a vehicle for people to get in touch with people who represented their companies, thereby personalizing their brand experience. Then it became a way for individuals to establish their own personal brand by documenting their conversations.

   Now Twitter is changing into a new way to disseminate news. Around the world it is used as a tool for people with no other outlet to report on what is happening on their street, in their town, or inside their country. It personalizes news and will continue to do so.

2   **Real-time customer support.** For business it is doing the same thing. Customers now expect to be able to find and communicate with their favorite brands and companies on Twitter. It used to be a novelty for someone to find you there, now it's annoying for someone not to be able to find you there. That's the future – an expectation of real-time updates from your business. There really is no wrong way to do it, but it is wrong not to do it at all.

TWITTER TOOLS AND RESOURCES

SOCIAL OOMPH

Goofy name but fantastic service that allows you to automate many of the repetitive features on Twitter and schedule updates to happen later.

MARKETMESUITE.COM

Marketmesuite is one of several "Twitter clients" that helps you organize and better utilize Twitter through your computer desktop, rather than through the clunkier and very basic Twitter.com website.

WEFOLLOW (WWW.WEFOLLOW.COM)

WeFollow is a directory of people on Twitter, sort of like a Twitter phone book. It will help you find people in different areas that you are interested in.

BIT.LY (WWW.BIT.LY)

This is a URL shortening service that allows you to track links. They have a very easy account set up process. You can cut and paste long URLs and they will shorten them to under 20 characters. No matter where you put that URL, all of the clicks are tracked with real-time analytics under your account on their website.

Facebook

🗨 INTRODUCTION

With over 500 million registered users and more than 60 million daily status updates, Facebook has an enormous reach for any social media marketing campaign. While there are some privacy concerns, Facebook is set up for people to share things that they like with their friends – a marketer's dream.

With Facebook you can have two kinds of pages, a personal profile and a business page. I recommend setting both up – the personal page for yourself and the business page for your product/service/company. In this section I will focus on setting up a page for your business. To do this you will need to set up a personal page first. Facebook makes the process easy, and you can start right now.

FACEBOOK BASICS

SETTING UP YOUR FACEBOOK PAGE

- Step 1: Go to www.facebook.com/pages/create.php
- Step 2: Choose what kind of page you want to set up. Most likely you will choose "Brand, product, or organization." "Local business" is for a mom-and-pop operation and "Artist, band or public figure" is for just what it says.
- Step 3: Identify your "Product." Facebook will provide you with a dropdown menu of options. Choose the most appropriate.
- Step 4: Create your page. Enter a name for your page (e.g. Your Company) and check the box that you are authorized to create this page. Then click "Create Official Page."

Your page will instantly be created. Now comes the good part – you get to personalize it and turn it into something that represents your brand.

BRANDING YOUR PAGE

- Step 1: Add a picture. Hover the mouse over the question mark in the upper left corner of the page. Click on it and it takes you to your photo page. You don't have anything there yet, so click on "Change Profile Picture."

   From there you will get a screen that allows you to upload a picture from your computer. Choose one that is square or close to square, as you will need to crop the image to make it fit in the box that Facebook provides.

- Step 2: Add Basic Info. Just under the picture, there is a section that reads: "Write Something about Your Company." Click on those words and a blank text box will come up. In this box write a one sentence description of your product/service/company. Then write another sentence about what the purpose of your Facebook page is so that people know what to do when they are on the page.
- Step 3: Edit Info tab. At the top of the screen there is a series of tabs. Click on the "Info" tab. Then click "Edit Information." In this section you will be able to add your founding date in the "Basic Info section." Under "Detailed Info" you can add links to your website, a brief company overview, your mission statement and a brief overview of your products.
- Step 4: Edit Photos tab. Click on the "Photos" tab. This tab allows you to create different galleries of photos. I recommend creating a gallery that showcases your product/service in action, and a second gallery that has you or people you work for interacting. The first gallery will give your visitors images of what you do and the second images that humanize your brand.
- Step 5: Edit Discussions tab. Click on the "Discussions" tab. In here you can begin discussions like a chat room. It's a good place to ask questions like "How do you use our product?" or "What new products would you like to see?"
- Step 6: Add Video tab. Click on the "+" sign at the end of the tabs. Click on "Video." This will allow you to upload videos of yourself talking about your product or introducing yourself to your customers.

- Step 7: Add Notes tab. Click on the "+" sign again and click on "Notes." Notes are like blog entries – when you write and publish them they are immediately posted on all of your fans' homepages. This can be a great way to keep people updated on new ideas, innovations, and changes within both your company and your industry.
- Step 8: Add Events tab. Click once more on the "+" sign and click on "Events." This will allow you to create event invitations for events you want your fans to attend, or online happenings that you create about your product/service/company.

EXAMPLE

COCA-COLA (WWW.FACEBOOK.COM/COCACOLA)

One of the largest companies in the world has not only one of the best Facebook fan pages, but one of the best stories behind that page. If you go there, you'll find an extremely engaging page with a beautiful custom Welcome tab. You'll find thousands of comments every day and you'll find a commitment from Coca-Cola to keep their global brand healthy and alive. And the most wonderful part is that the page itself, with well over 10 million fans, was started not by the company but by two fans who loved Coke and wanted them to have a presence on Facebook. And what did Coca-Cola do when they found this out? Did they try to push the two aside and take over the fan page? No. In true social media fashion, Coca-Cola flew the page administrators to the Coca-Cola corporate headquarters in Atlanta and started working alongside them to keep the conversation going.

ADVANCED USES OF FACEBOOK

- **Facebook Ads:** Once you have started a Facebook fan page for your business and have a consistent posting schedule, some interaction and a fan base, promoting that page through Facebook Ads to grow your fan numbers makes a lot of sense.
- **Contests and polls:** After the initial wave of getting people you know and big fans of your business or product to "Like" your fan page, you'll need to do something to keep them engaged. I recommend holding contests, asking questions, or holding polls on the fan page. There are a number of services available to help you set these up and track the results.
- **FBML:** Facebook Markup Language (FBML) is like HTML, the programming language, but adapted to work on Facebook. FBML is an application that you can add to your Facebook page that will allow you to create custom pictures, links and messaging for new tabs that you can also create. While not completely as versatile as a website, you have a significantly larger number of options and it makes any tab highly customizable.

 ## WHAT THE FUTURE HOLDS

PLACES

Facebook entered the location-based arena in the summer of 2010, and with their 500 million people, the use of the service is sure both to expand and redefine what the location-based services are capable of doing. Facebook already has a massive amount of data from user profiles that they use to make advertisements very targeted – expect them to make the same kind of targeting available to businesses based on the locations that Facebook users frequent.

CONNECT

Facebook Connect is already utilized widely around the web for people to register or log in to a variety of sites and networks. This will grow, and I think it will grow to be used for payments. Facebook is integrating everything from gaming to shopping.

"LIKE" BUTTONS

In 2010 Facebook also introduced "Like" buttons to be used anywhere on the Internet, not just in Facebook. These "Like" buttons will be integrated into Facebook's ability to help marketers target preferences. Like "Places" and "Connect," the Facebook "Like" buttons are an incredible source of information for marketers.

 FACEBOOK TOOLS AND RESOURCES

INSIDE FACEBOOK WWW.INSIDEFACEBOOK.COM/

This blog is focused on everything new you need to know as it happens for developers and marketers – it gets deep into Facebook.

FACEBOOK BADGE WWW.FACEBOOK.COM/BADGES/

This is a simple badge that you can use to promote your Facebook fan page. People can add it to their pages anywhere on the Internet, and it links back to your Facebook page. It's a great way to get some visibility and increase traffic.

FACEBOOK INSIGHTS

Get to know the analytics that Facebook provides for your page – the metrics, charts and numbers they track for you are impressive, and are all available to you for free. To get there, just click "See all" under "Insights" on the left column of your fan page.

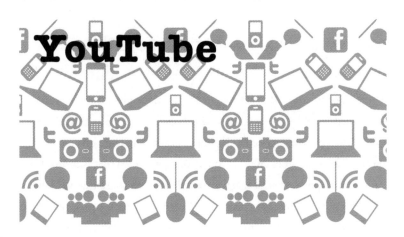

YouTube

INTRODUCTION

YouTube is just what it says – you on the tube. By now you've heard of it – the basic concept is that anyone can make a video and upload it to the Internet. Popular videos get anywhere from tens of thousands to tens of millions of views, each one the envy of any and every marketer.

It was founded by three employees of PayPal in 2005. They registered the domain name on Feb 15, 2005 and by December they had venture capital funding and took the company live. From there they continued growing and were eventually purchased by Google.

YOUTUBE BASICS

For marketing, YouTube is important because it gives any person or company the ability to reach customers or potential customers through video. There are a few key ways in which YouTube can expand your ability to reach your target market.

KEY WAYS TO EXPAND YOUR TARGET MARKET

1   Viral video

Viral video means a lot of different things, depending on who you ask. The word "viral" is taken from medical parlance. A virus spreads exponentially as people exposed to the virus pass it on. The same idea is true with a video that "goes viral." If you can create a video that is entertaining or has an important message, people will want to share that video with their friends, family and colleagues. In this way, you can spread your marketing message in an entertaining fashion, giving you a wide exposure as the video is passed from person to person through people that they trust. Coming from someone they know, they will trust the message in that video more than if they saw it as a commercial or on your website.

2   Vlog

Vlog is short for Video Blog. YouTube allows people or companies to create videos, and stringing those videos together or creating a group of videos around a central theme can be a powerful way to convey your messaging through video. There have been many Vlog celebrities with wildly popular Vlogs, essentially creating their own television shows that are disseminated through YouTube. While your product or service may not have the entertainment value that many of the popular Vloggers do, you can still reach your target audience with a series that presents your messaging in an entertaining way. Incorporating video into your company blog or creating a separate YouTube channel is yet another way that YouTube can get your content out there.

3   Interviews

A YouTube channel for your company or service allows you to hold conversations with other prominent people in your industry. I use short video interviews as a way to connect with other people in the marketing industry and introduce them to people on my blog. One of the key features of doing this means that the people you meet at conferences will want to see the video or interview you make of them, so that creates traffic for your blog. Not only that, there is a good chance that they will want other people to see their interview. If they pass an interview on with a link, or even embed your interview into their blog, you have the seed of a viral video.

4   Personalization

Making videos of yourself to post on YouTube allows you to personalize your business, product or service. People will then have a way to put a face and a voice to what it is that you do – and that can let them feel that they know you and what you do even better than just reading about it on your website.

 HOW TO USE IT IN PRACTICE

YouTube makes it easy to set up an account and post videos.

- Step 1: Create a video and save it in .mp4 or .mov format. When you create your video keep in mind that YouTube has a ten minute time limit, so keep your video somewhere under that.
- Step 2: Go to YouTube.com.
- Step 3: Open a user account and follow the instructions.
- Step 4: Click on "Upload" at the top of the screen.
- Step 5: Click on the yellow "Upload Video" button, choose the video from your computer, and click "Open" or "Save." As they say, your video can be:

- High Definition
- Up to 2 GB in size.
- Up to 10 minutes in length.

- Step 6: Name your video. In this step, use your personal name, the name of your company, or the name of your product. If you can fit all three, do it.
- Step 7: Tags. Just like you are writing a blog entry, you want to add the keywords you use across the web for your product/service/company.
- Step 8: Description. It's important to use keywords in your extended descriptions here as well. But also, make sure that your description is to the point. Only the first 100 characters or so will appear beneath your video, so keep your basic description to one concise sentence.

EXTENDED USE CASE …

For many small business and marketing bloggers, you'll want to use your videos in as many places as possible. If you are a blogger, you want to use video on your blogs. It has the advantage of personalizing your interview, giving a face to the two voices and, if you are talking about a product, you can turn that product over in your hands, giving a 3-D visual that is much more relatable than the 2-D classic advertisements.

EXAMPLE

LONELYGIRL15

LonelyGirl15 was one of the first and more successful uses of YouTube as a viral marketing vehicle. Jessica Lee Rose, an American-New

Zealand actress, posed as a 19-year-old home-schooled girl. At first it was presented as if the character, "Bree," was a real person. As time went on, people became suspicious of LonelyGirl15 being a hoax or a promotional ploy, and the character garnered a lot of press as people tried to figure out if she was real or not. The producers behind the hoax used the publicity to very successfully launch a web series. Eventually, LonelyGirl15 also became one of the first series to utilize product placement. They featured both Hershey's Icebreaker's Sours Gum and Neutrogena products in the web series.

GENERAL HOW-TO VIDEOS

YouTube is full of how-to videos, for everything from applying make-up to how to pick a lock. Creating one of these can cut your customer service needs, create more exposure for your product, and give bloggers and other members of the press easy access to a demo of what you do or create.

 ADVANCED USES OF YOUTUBE

TAGS

When you are uploading a video onto YouTube, the "tags" section is extremely important. Not only does it allow people to find your video, but it sets the stage for where your video will show up in the Google search function. Consider your keywords here carefully, focusing on what you want people to find your video for. In most cases, people will not search for a company or product by name, especially if you are not a big brand. What people do search for are How-To videos or Best Of videos. If you can figure out a crossover with one of those kind of videos or a way to create videos about your business that fit that format, do it. And then tag it appropriately.

VIDEO PROMOTION

YouTube has a featured video section on their homepage. They feature some videos based on what the editors like, and you can submit your video for consideration to be featured. If you can make a video that stands out, is well made and has some kind of unique feature, you will increase your chances of being featured.

PRODUCT PLACEMENT

If your product is something that people could feature in a video, it could be to your advantage to find Vloggers with large YouTube followings of subscribers and donate your product for use. Alternatively, finding Vloggers who are speaking to your niche market is equally effective.

 ## WHAT THE FUTURE HOLDS

YouTube continues to gain on traditional television. In the future, I expect it to become as important, if not more so, than other broadcast mediums. Recently they laid claim to actually getting more viewers during prime time than mainstream television did. This means that people are turning to web video, and especially YouTube, to choose what they want to watch. Because YouTube allows people to purchase ad space at the bottom of their videos, identifying what your target audience is watching enables you to get your message to those people in much the same way that traditional television advertising did.

YouTube continues to play a big role in any kind of performing art, like music or dance. It is easily shareable and has helped stars like Lady Gaga and Soulja Boy achieve much faster rises to popularity than would have been possible with only traditional media available – possibly enabling them to become the stars they are in the first place.

YOUTUBE TOOLS AND RESOURCES

A MAC

If you are really serious about making videos, especially for the web, it's the perfect excuse to switch over to the Apple world. An Apple MacBook will come with build in video software that will make it easy for you to create and edit footage.

FLIP VIDEO

If you are a Blackberry devotee, your best option for creating video that's easy to upload is to get a Flip video camera. A good model will cost $150–$200 and it will make professional-quality video that is simple to upload to your YouTube account.

LINKEDIN

💬 INTRODUCTION

L inkedIn is a social media network created specifically for business relationships, especially around job search. It's a place where, in a sense, resumés come alive and speak to each other. It's a place to find a job or find employees, but most important, it can be a hub for your business history on the Internet.

💻 LINKEDIN BASICS

LinkedIn is a social network specifically aimed at people in professional careers. It has three main functions:

1   JOB SEARCH

This can work both ways. People looking for a job will use LinkedIn to look for other people who are in their field and try to make a connection. With free accounts you can't send a message to someone you're not connected to already, but you can find out some basic information, and you can send a request to get connected. Along with that request, you can personalize your message to start a conversation.

In the ongoing job search market, LinkedIn serves as a living resumé. People can update their LinkedIn account and keep an active list of what they have done and what they are doing. You can link your Twitter account so that what you are doing on that network becomes part of your LinkedIn page as well.

2 PROFESSIONAL GROUPS

One of the key ways people connect on LinkedIn is through the Groups. Because LinkedIn is aimed at professionals, the Groups are organized around what people do in their careers. This is an ideal way to meet and form relationships with other people in your field and industry. Through those connections, business partnerships can be started, personal brands created, and you can keep yourself abreast of everything new that is happening in your industry.

3 PARTNERSHIP CONNECTIONS

LinkedIn has a feature that keeps track of what degree of connection you have to the people on your list – 1st, 2nd, and 3rd. It will suggest other people that you are connected to through your current connections. You could very well discover that you are connected to someone through a former or current colleague, and when you need to reach out and work with someone new, you can ask your colleague to introduce you. Beyond that, LinkedIn has a feature where you can write references for people you have worked with and they can write references for you. In this way, you can utilize your network to create an ongoing set of references from people in a very public space. When others are looking at your online life, these recommendations can prove a powerful way to represent yourself as trustworthy and a good person to do business with.

HOW TO USE IT IN PRACTICE

LinkedIn is about establishing and maintaining business relationships – not about hosting your resumé online. Remember this when you begin setting up your profile and thinking about how to use the network available.

That said, here is how you get started:

- Step 1: Visit the homepage and fill out the "Join Today" box. When you choose an email address to use, make sure it is the one that you primarily use for business, as this is where your updates will go.
- Step 2: Enter basic information about where you live and work and what company you work for. LinkedIn will auto-fill the fields where you enter your company information – this will work to your advantage later when you want to connect with other people in your company.
- Step 3: Enter your email address. Go through the steps to authenticate your email address. Make sure to remember your chosen password, as you will need to log in when it brings you back from the email message.
- Step 4: LinkedIn will then suggest people you may know based on the information you've already entered. I propose reaching out to all of the people they suggest that you do recognize.

- Step 5: Complete your profile. Once you put in this basic information, you will be able to go to the Profile tab on the top menu bar. LinkedIn makes it very easy and straightforward to find where to fill in the rest of your information. It can take a while to do this, so allot at least an hour when you want to go in and create your account. You don't want to start, invite people to connect with you, and then leave your account close to empty because you get busy. There is a bar with a percentage on the right side of the page that will tell you how "complete" your profile is.

- Step 6: Answers. When you have your profile filled out, click on the Home tab in the top menu bar. On the lower right-hand part of the screen is the "Answers" section, where people in related fields have asked questions. I recommend this to be one of the first things you do to get yourself involved in the community.

ADVANCED USES

GIVE AND ASK FOR RECOMMENDATIONS

Once you have your profile filled out, LinkedIn will probably still not list your profile as 100% completed. You'll need to get recommendations from other people who are on LinkedIn. I love that they consider this as part of the way that you fill out your profile, rather than as an add-on that is used later. It speaks to the inherent social nature of LinkedIn, and the emphasis on relationships.

The first step in getting recommendations is giving them. Use the people search function to find others you've worked with. LinkedIn will scan your email contacts, and that's the best way to get started. After that, start searching for names of people you have worked with in the past or currently worked with that you respect and have a good relationship with. These could also be people you've met on Twitter that you've created partnerships with. Write up recommendations for those people. Some of them will offer to write a recommendation for you back. Alternately, follow up with them a few days later and ask if they would be willing to write one for you, but keep in mind that not everyone is comfortable doing this. Don't take it personally if they choose not to recommend you.

ANSWER QUESTIONS

LinkedIn has many industry-specific chat rooms and groups. People will often ask questions or start discussions around things they are learning about or trying to figure out. Answering these questions frequently is a great way to position yourself as an expert in your field, and it will come in handy later on when you are looking to connect with new people if they recognize your picture and name from industry groups.

 WHAT THE FUTURE HOLDS

LinkedIn has established itself as the go-to resource for people to look for and vet new talent for new hires or partnerships. The user-base will continue to grow, and become more and more important as people entering the workplace utilize LinkedIn to build their online and social media resumé.

With the world economy continuing to be difficult, I envision the new strategies for how people connect and cultivate those connections starting or codifying on LinkedIn. Understanding how people are using LinkedIn to pursue or maintain business relationships will remain critical.

 TOOLS AND RESOURCES

LinkedIn does not have the kind of tools or add-ons that other social networks have, but there are some good places to stay up on what's new in the LinkedIn world and learn how to use the network:

- **LinkedIn webinars:** (www.learn.linkedin.com/training/). They actually run a great series of their own LinkedIn webinars that will give you the basics and help you create it.
- **LinkedIntelligence Blog:** (www.linkedintelligence.com/). Billed as "The unofficial source for all things LinkedIn," the updates are incredibly helpful in making LinkedIn work for you and your business.

Chapter 2
Digital Branding

"The intangible sum of a product's attributes: its name, packaging, and price, its history, its reputation, and the way it's advertised."

David Ogilvy's definition of "brand"

 INTRODUCTION

Branding is increasingly important in the era of online marketing and social media. When we want to buy something we can choose from companies in a globally competitive market. In the days of *Mad Men*, companies stated their brand and consumers believed in the brand. Those days are gone. People still trust people but they no longer trust companies.

Now brand perceptions are increasingly made by you and me – the consumers. A large part of a brand is made up of the customer experience of it. Brands are made on the front line by the way in which company staff interact with their customers. Customers share their experiences – good or bad – with all the other potential and existing customers via social media. This being the case the personal brands of the individuals within/representing the company become important. Companies hire people with good personal brands and do not hire those with indecent photos on their Facebook walls.

A company's brand is its essence. While the term "branding" is a buzzword that gets thrown around online to mean pretty much anything – from an employee's tweet to a large advertising campaign – the key aspect of digital branding is that it is the sum of everyone's perspectives, not just what a company says about itself.

The concept of corporate branding started to take hold in the post-WWII era alongside new mass media like radio and television. For several decades, it was the role of advertisers and marketers to convey what they wanted to be the "essence" of a product or company. The most common branding strategy was to broadcast a message across media channels, essentially telling consumers what to think about a brand. It worked well for generations – as long as consumers couldn't harness the same mediums to offer up their opinions to a wide audience.

With the Internet came an entirely new way for consumers to communicate with companies, and the concept and practice of digital branding was born. Traditional branding communication is not based on relationships, and it certainly isn't interactive. Digital branding is about creating the meaning of a brand through a much more interactive, relationship-based process. In many cases, what consumers say about and do with a product is more important than what the company does.

With digital branding, a company is part of an ongoing and constantly changing conversation that fluidly defines their brand. You've probably heard that companies no longer "own their brand." In some ways, they never did. And it's certainly true in the sense that a company can't treat its brand like something they keep hidden in a safe and trot out when they want to make a statement. Rather than think that companies don't own their brand, though, it's more accurate to say that they have become co-owners, along with everyone else in the digital space.

Companies still set the tone and play a critical role in their branding. If digital branding is based on conversation, relationships and interaction, a company needs to be conversing, relating and interacting. As part of that evolving conversation, companies have begun developing more personality-focused brands because consumers relate better to people and characters than to corporate entities.

At the same time, branding is not just for companies and products anymore. An entirely new field of "personal branding" is growing in importance, both for individuals and for the businesses where they work. An individual's personal brand is the essence of who they are in relation to the work that they do.

And whether the brand is corporate or personal, brand reputation management is a challenge.

In this chapter I'll discuss the basics of digital branding for a company or product, look at the evolving importance of personal branding, and outline the ways either a company or an individual can proactively manage their digital brand.

 ## THE BASICS

YOUR COMPANY

In the era of digital branding, your brand is the lens through which the consumer and the company interact. How your company presents itself, how people perceive your company, and how all of those interactions distill together, creates the essence of your brand.

There have been four important shifts in how companies approach branding from a digital perspective:

1   How you are defined
2   How you communicate
3   How you interact
4   How you deliver

1 How you are defined

Just a decade ago, most brands were defined through advertising and marketing efforts. These days, that is just one piece of the puzzle. Advertising and marketing both make up some of the digital branding arsenal, but you are no longer defined strictly by what you say about yourself. You are defined by what other people are saying about you on social networks, on blogs, and on the other media they make. You are defined by your own company's presence on those digital fronts. If you are there, you are part of your digital brand – if not, others will speak for you and your brand will be made without your input if you are not engaged.

2 How you communicate

This is both what you use and how you use it. Blogs are a great example, because companies use them in a variety of ways. Some CEOs or VPs have their own blogs where they keep a running dialogue with people about their ideas and their take on their industry. These writers approach their digital brand to be a thought leader. That's one way to do it, and it makes your brand stand out, as there aren't a whole lot of CEOs who take the time to write a blog.

Other brands are utilizing social networks as an entirely new way to communicate. Having a group of people on social networks like Twitter or Facebook makes the communication between customers and executives more personal, and while most people will not approach an executive there, many more will look at what those executives are tweeting or posting about.

Digital branding humanizes your executives – people can relate to a brand when they find that the people behind it are, well, people – just like them.

3 How you interact

This is one of the biggest fears of the people I work with. "What if we get on Twitter and people say bad things about our brand? What do we do? What if people start complaining to me about this or that?" No matter who you are, that's going to happen – just like in any other medium. Social media and the process of digital branding is not a happy rainbow place where everything is always great and everyone sings songs together in the park. It is the kind of place where everything is public, and sometimes things do get nasty. But this is much more of an opportunity than a problem or something to fear. The fact that everything is public lets your brand, again, be human about responding to complaints or problems.

Think about the last time you saw two people in an argument, or the last time you were in an argument. Was it the person complaining or the person who dealt with the complaint in a calm, helpful way who came out looking the best? If people complain or shoot daggers on the Internet, giving them a positive response and actually helping them to solve their problem will do wonders for your digital branding. Comcast created a Twitter account (@comcastcares) for just this kind of customer service reason, and it worked. Not only do people loathe cable TV service, but they often have something to say about the installation or the actual day-to-day service. By creating a Twitter account to make their customer service public, Comcast turned the perception of their company as one full of problems on its head. They dealt with those problems out in the public eye, and came to be known as the brand that does care.

4 How you deliver

Deliver your products and services well and your customers will check in on Foursquare or Facebook and share their delight. However there is no marketing cure for delivery that sucks. If your products and services do not work then no matter how good your marketing, people will not buy your produces or services and they will share your poor delivery with potential customers. A YouTube video of your McDonald's server spitting in your bun before you get it will reverberate around the Internet faster than any viral video marketing video you could create.

PERSONAL BRANDING WITHIN YOUR COMPANY

If people still trust people but not companies then the personal brands of the people in the company are increasingly important. Individuals with positive and extensive personal brands are assets to the company.

Personal branding is about creating and maintaining the essence of *you* in the digital space. An effective Internet presence represents *you* to customers, clients, and potential partners in a way that keeps you relevant and amazing. Did I say amazing? Yes. As Seth Godin says in his book *Linchpin*, the way to get and keep a job is to be indispensible. In digital branding, you don't want people to see you and say, "Yeah, that's nice ..." you want them to see your tweet, read your blog or read your profile and say, "That's Amazing!" And that's what I'm talking about.

In some ways, personal branding is like packaging yourself. That packaging manages expectations and impressions of other people both within and outside your company. I'm going to talk about how you can create and build your own personal brand as part of the marketing department within your company. Many of the same principles will work for individuals looking for work, working as freelancers or consultants, or simply looking to make a move in their field.

HOW TO USE IT IN PRACTICE

Branding strategy is interactive and fluid, not a message you slap on a billboard and walk away from. Brand identity in the digital sense is active. Because the Internet is a public place, your brand is a public figure. Think of it the way you think of dressing up a child for school – you give them clothes, advice and directions, but once they head out into the world (the Internet), you can't control what other people are going to think of them, or what kind of situation they will end up being in. When your child comes back at the end of the day, he's had an entire set of experiences that are now part of his life. It's the same with a digital brand – every day a brand is out there it is having interactions with web surfers, advertisements, bloggers, and social networks, it is changing dynamically, far from the hands of the traditional brand manager.

Digital branding is about creating an effective Internet presence that will allow your company to stay involved with the brand that you are no longer solely in charge of. For this reason, the brand you create needs to be honest. You want your brand messaging to be about the essence and the core of your company, similar to a mission statement – not about trying to sell things. It needs to be about what matters most to you and to your company, and hopefully that is what you consistently deliver.

As Chris Brogan says, "the differentiator on brands is in what you deliver." Very true. A brand will be transparently judged in the digital space based on whether it delivers on what it says. What you do and how you are in turn defines your brand as much as what you say you are in your advertising and marketing – in fact, the real-time opinions of your customers and potential customers may be more important than what your corporate messaging has to say.

DIGITAL BRANDING FOCUS

With digital branding, there are three things to focus on. I like to think of them as three things that you need to "get" to create an effective digital branding strategy. Tactics come later.

1   Get noticed
2   Get innovative
3   Get relationships

Sure, it's easy to list out. Sure, create a unique and endlessly innovative brand that has real relationships with customers. Right.

How about Starbucks? How about Coke? How about your favorite restaurant? How about Wal-Mart? Do customers actually have a relationship with these companies? Some do. But at all of these places, customers do have relationships with employees that work there, and in turn with the brand itself. You yourself do not have to have that relationship with every single customer. Your job is to create the tools for the people on both sides, your customers and your employees, to have those relationships. And to do that and keep people interested, you need to be unique and stand out – meaning, you need to get noticed. To stay noticed, you need to be innovative. And, remember, the reason you are doing both of those things is to build and sustain relationships with your customers where your brand truly exits. Thinking back to the definition of branding as the sum of a brand's intangible attributes, the essence of that brand, this is where you do the work to improve your intangible attributes, where you communicate and live out that essence.

You've probably heard the phrase "content is king," and while this is often the case on the Internet in general, in digital branding, content isn't so much king as it is the currency that allows everything else to happen. Content is the way that people get and stay connected. You need to create relationships through content in context.

That content needs to make your brand remarkable, and to be remarkable you need to be innovative. If you can keep your brand remarkable and innovative, you'll have dynamic relationships that will keep your brand presence in the digital space where it needs to be.

Content is the conduit through which your company defines itself, communicates and reacts. Your company can digitally brand itself in a positive or negative light, to be sure, using these principles. But you want to brand yourself in a positive light – so where do you start?

WHERE TO START

1   GET NOTICED

How do you get yourself noticed online? It's a lot like going to a party where you don't know anyone – although depending on the size of your company, plenty of people may already know you. If they do, then just showing up is going to get you noticed by some people. If that's the case for you, be ready with your strategy before you start setting up any social networking accounts. Accounts with "radio-silence" can have a much worse effect on a digital branding reputation than not having an account at all.

Blogging and social networking are two critical ways for a company to be active in the creation of their digital brand. But it's not about jumping in just because you think you should be there. The first step is to think about who your audience is and what the purpose of your digital brand will be. It's about knowing what story you want to tell and about deciding where and how to tell that story.

To get noticed, first decide who you want to notice you. The failure of many traditional marketing and advertising venues has been that they broadcast their message to everyone, hoping that the right people will notice. In digital branding, targeting your messaging is important. You'll want to take a survey of the social media and blogging options and decide where the people you want to reach are, as that is where you want a presence.

2 GET INNOVATIVE

And that's where the innovation starts. The Internet itself, and social networking in particular, is still relatively new – you know that, otherwise you wouldn't be reading this. Doing what everyone else is doing isn't going to work. People are looking for something new and exciting, or new and simple, or new and reliable. But the key is to offer something that uses the tools everyone else is using in an innovative way. Don't copy – this is *your* brand you are creating.

3 GET RELATIONSHIPS

Relationships grow when people do things together. One of the best ways to create and build relationships with your customers is to do things together. Luckily, social media makes that a very accessible option. For example, Facebook Fan Pages give you almost constant contact with your fans. Instead of broadcasting messages on your website or writing and waiting for comments on a blog, Fan Pages allow you to post and respond to your fans in real-time, create quizzes and polls to keep your fans engaged, and allow you to have extended, public conversations with people who already "Like" your brand.

Once you understand those three pillars – getting noticed, getting innovative and getting relationships, it's time to start building your brand.

WHAT TO DO

Building your brand

1   **Digital audit.** Take an inventory of where your company already is online – both what you say about yourself and what others are saying about you. You may want to enlist a social media monitoring service if there is a lot of content about you already. Note: I suggest five good monitoring tools at the end of the chapter.

2   **Alignment.** From here, check with your company mission statement and any recent interviews by executives (or yourself). Look for what is out there that you want to be out there, and what your company defines itself as that isn't out there yet. Both are opportunities to increase focus on your brand, whether it is reinforcing what is already out there, or getting what's missing out into the digital space.

3   **Awareness.** Once you know what you want to say and where you want to be (digitally), it's time to make sure you are there and all of your messaging is set. Align your bios and profiles and everything else that goes along with social media and blogging accounts, ensuring that it is consistent and in line with the brand you want to project.

Building your relationships

1   **Listen.** Now that you have created the digital channels to talk and figured out what you want to say, it's time to listen. You'll be tempted to get out there and start talking about yourself and your

company right away, but the point of listening is so that you get the lie of the land first. It's like walking into a party and surveying the room before you just burst in and start talking to the first person you meet. Find out who the influencers are, find out when and where your customers and potential customers spend their online time. Those are the conversations you want to join and work your branding messaging into.

2 **Interact.** Yes, there is interaction. You're living your story as a brand representative for your company, and it's time to start telling and creating that story. When you join conversations, remember that you are not a salesperson, you are not an advertisement, and you are not a person simply relaying the message from within your company. You are a living, breathing conduit for the content and messaging that is your company. The messaging is not the brand, the digital accounts are not the brand – how you interact with people and relay that messaging is what will determine the brand. Like they told you when you were a kid – be yourself.

3 **Stay in touch.** Digital branding is just like any other kind of relationship – it's easy to fall out of touch, even when you've made a good connection. This doesn't mean start a big spreadsheet of all the people you interact with (or maybe it does, depending on how you do things). What it means is that you stay active on the computer every day, you write the blog, you interact on Twitter, and you update the rest of your content.

Building your outreach

1 **Sharing.** Some of the media you create should be ready-made for sharing. Anything on YouTube or your blog should be easy to share on Twitter and Facebook, or Tumblr and Flickr. The point is, if you make something that other people want to share, make

it easy on them. And don't be afraid to directly ask people that are your work colleagues or work for companies you work with to share the content you create. In some ways, it's the classic "I'll scratch your back if you scratch mine." Part of your digital strategy is sharing others' content, and it's OK to ask them, nicely, to share yours.

2   **Ambassadors promote the brand.** People will share what you create, if you create it well and stay human and relatable inside your company's brand. Be ready for it. It will make you responsible for even more relationships, and it's important to support and encourage the people who come to light as ambassadors in your digital world. Be thankful, and show it.

PERSONAL DIGITAL BRANDING

It's a similar process to doing it for your company, but the key difference is that you are doing it within the context of your company. If you find yourself wanting to make a career move or a shift within your company, this process takes on even more importance, as it shows, in a real-time way, what you have to offer, and what your unique value is.

1   Define yourself

Decide and understand what you are passionate about. Of course, this is easier said than done, and hopefully you're already doing it, but if you're not sure and you're not there, this is where you start. Tailor your passion to create a niche, whether that's within your company or within the online space.

2   Brand yourself

- **Job title.** Within your company, you probably already have a job title. It's important for that job title to fit with and describe what you actually do and how you define yourself. Make sure this is true. Then create business cards that define you that way.

- **Blogging.** If your company has a blog, start writing for it. Even if you are writing from within the voice of your company, your personal voice and signature on consistent, fresh media that is searchable online will be a valuable way to start building your personal brand within the company.

- **Twitter.** Depending on your company's social media policy, Twitter is a great way to start building your personal digital brand. If your company is still closed off to social media, it will take some work converting them, and you should start at the top, convincing the decision-makers.

- **Video.** You want people to see you being you. Make a short video introducing yourself and make sure it is connected to all of your online accounts. If the blog is your own, make it available on the homepage. The more people have the ability to relate to you as a real person (and not just a resumé), the more they will do so.

- **Evangelize.** Start talking about digital branding to others in your office and at your company. You'll be amazed at the conversations that start, the little pieces of information that people know and want to share, and at how quickly you become the go-to person for digital branding advice and knowledge. And when you're the go-to person, you learn and grow even faster than the people you are teaching.

EXAMPLES OF DIGITAL BRANDING

PEPSI REFRESH: WWW.REFRESHEVERYTHING.COM

Coke has long had a strong brand that is woven into the fabric of cultures and communities around the world. They've always had strong advertising presence, and have expanded around the world. They are part of memories.

Pepsi, while the second-leading cola brand in the world, has focused on celebrity endorsements and pop-culture ads for most of its existence. In 2010 they embraced a bold new presence through their Pepsi Refresh campaign. In this campaign they have boldly used social networking sites, from Twitter to Facebook to Foursquare, to promote their campaign and put their money where their mouth is, shifting their Super Bowl advertising budget from buying television spots to use it all as part of this purely digital campaign.

The concept is that they are "giving away millions each month to fund refreshing ideas that change the world." No small goal. Anyone can submit an idea in a variety of categories, and anyone can vote on the idea that they like best. Pepsi gives money to the winners.

Brand awareness? Check. Innovation? Check. Building relationships? Check. Positive brand ambassadors to evangelize their brand? You'd better believe it.

Giving away money to good causes that their fans and customers choose is a genius way for Pepsi to position themselves as the kind of brand that not only cares, but gets involved. And it is a sure-fire way to create brand ambassadors – whether the people who receive the money drink Pepsi or not, they will be talking about Pepsi in relation to something they are passionate about. That's good digital branding.

TRUMP (DONALD, OF COURSE!): WWW.TRUMP.COM

When I hear the name Trump, I think of business and money. He wrote a book called *The Art of the Deal*. The Trump Towers are named after him. He runs a show called *The Apprentice*. I think, this guy knows how to build a brand. Have all of his business ventures been successful? No. But the fact is that whilst Trump has declared bankruptcy in some of his ventures, and is by no means the richest or shrewdest businessperson in the world, he knows how to position himself, and that makes him one of the best branded.

Through his television show, books, and entrepreneur initiatives, he is constantly creating relationships. His name is out there. His name is attached to things that define who he is. And he proactively defines himself with these things – and then acts on it, creating ongoing interactions.

 ADVANCED USES IN DIGITAL BRANDING

1 LOCAL BRANDING INFLUENCE

Digital branding is often thought of as something big because it can reach across and around the entire Internet. But once you have the presence, a big part of building the relationships and ambassadors who will perpetuate and ultimately help define your brand is connecting with people and other companies in a one-on-one basis.

There are events going on in your city or town. Sponsor them. But don't just pay money to throw your name on some of the literature and have it announced at some ceremony. Take time out of your day and make it your business to meet the organizers, go to some parts of the event, and bring someone along to record your meetings. Blog about who you meet, what they're doing, and why your company is sponsoring the event. Do this during the week or two leading up to the event and do it during the event.

People respond to relationships, and they respond when someone they didn't expect to come and visit comes and gives them credit or pays attention. When you tell those stories through your company website, blog, and social media channels, you are creating a message of care, and showing evidence of relationships. Send the media you create to the people at the events and they will share it with their networks, and they will talk about you. And before you know it, you've created ambassadors for your company.

2   DIGITAL BRANDING WHITEPAPERS

A whitepaper is an authoritative report or guide that is often oriented toward a particular issue or problem. A whitepaper is a powerful tool for extending your company's influence in a particular field. At the same time, a whitepaper about how you assessed, planned, and created your brand will not only solidify the fact that that is your brand, it will make your company (and you) a thought-leader in digital branding within your field. It will get other companies and other marketing managers looking at what you did for ideas, and that gets your name out there within your own industry.

WHAT THE FUTURE HOLDS FOR DIGITAL BRANDING

As digital branding continues to evolve and the tools that make it possible become more sophisticated, the ongoing conversation that creates your digital brand will equally become more sophisticated and complex. While relationships and conversations will remain at its core, I expect more and more best practices and standardized ways to establish a brand to come into being. More than anything, the simple fact that there are now branding consultants indicates that there is indeed a process and a system to creating the brand.

What won't change is that, at its core, branding is about humanizing your company or product and interacting with your consumer to establish a relationship. The stories you tell through your digital branding efforts will define who you are as a company and, in turn, will create and build the relationships you want to have with both current and potential customers. And when you tell a story, you make people part of that story – and when they are part of your story, they become ambassadors for that story. And that is how digital branding will grow.

> "What people say about you matters more than what you may say about yourself. Nobody is really credible to provide an honest perspective on himself.
> Entering the era of social media, inter-exchanges (i.e. communication between individuals) becomes more significant than the communications that you can have one on one.
> Let others talk about you. Let them use their own words. Use the consumer's dynamics.

The scale of the Internet, you can't trust everyone. Therefore you go for the ones you know. And frankly what you say matters less than who you are."

Bastien Beauchamp, Founder, The Bees Awards

TOOLS AND RESOURCES

There are a few blogs going that offer great information on branding as it evolves.

Brand New: www.underconsideration.com/brandnew

This blog offers a daily dose of opinions on corporate and brand identity work that will keep you thinking about your corporate brand.

David Young's Branding Blog: www.brandingblog.com

This blog is David's personal experiences and opinions on digital branding – he's passionate and honest and he keeps the human side of digital branding front and center.

Brand Architect: www.collings.co.za

Patrick Collings works with brands and companies in South Africa, and looks at branding from a holistic point of view.

Dan Schawbel's Personal Branding Blog: www.personalbrandingblog.com

This blog is an evolving guide based on his book Me 2.0 that helps you position yourself through marketing your passion and expertise.

William Arruda: www.williamarruda.com

This blog has an excellent personal and corporate branding perspective based on the idea that a brand is a "unique promise of value."

MONITORING TOOLS

Radian 6: www.radian6.com

"Radian6 was created with the idea that companies need to be listening to the social web in order to effectively participate. Intelligence about online conversations is critical: companies need to know what's being said about their brand, industry, and competitors online. So, we built a listening platform designed to help companies do just that."

– Radian 6, "About Us"

Alterian: www.alterian.com

"The Alterian platform combines campaign management, web content management, email and social media monitoring tools to help marketers be more insightful, engaging and accountable than ever before, by sending the best, most relevant message at the right time – regardless of channel. One of the key differentiators of the Alterian offering is that the various elements are integrated. The marketer can move seamlessly between organizing their resources, undertaking analytics, planning a campaign and overseeing the approvals necessary to drive things to timely completion."

– Alterain, "Our Company"

Trackur: www.trackur.com

"Trackur was created by online reputation management expert Andy Beal. The co-author of *Radically Transparent* – the first and only book available on online reputation management – Andy Beal is known around the world as the go-to-guy for reputation building, managing, and monitoring.

Frustrated that existing online reputation monitoring tools were either too complex or too expensive, Andy decided to create Trackur."

– Trackur, "About Trackur"

Brandwatch: www.brandwatch.com

"Brandwatch offers a full range of Social Media Monitoring tools and services. Whatever your needs, from a simple monitoring project to full-blown Analyst Reports or API integration, we have a solution for you."

– Brandwatch, "Monitoring tools"

Synthesio www.synthesio.com

"Synthesio is an international, multi-lingual web monitoring and research company helping brands and agencies find, collect, and make sense of the overwhelming data on the web."

– Synthesio, "About us"

Chapter 3
Company Websites

INTRODUCTION

Business is now as much online as it is in the boardroom, the storefront or the face-to-face meetings between executives. Your company website represents you online – it is the axis at the center of your web presence.

In the beginning (you know, say ten years ago ...) it was enough just to have a website but, increasingly, your website needs to be more than a static presence. With a growing proportion of business and interaction happening online, a company's website is a critical way to communicate with your customers and partner businesses.

Company websites are more than just the company brochure online. Your web-savvy and increasingly social users will expect news, real-time feeds, video and newsletter subscriptions with your site as the hub of your online activity. In essence, your website should connect any visitor to whatever they need to learn about, purchase from, or refer someone else to your business.

 ## THE BASICS

Why do I need a website at all again?

If you are reading this book, I expect you already realize that it's important for your business to have a website, but understanding why you have something is important. Just as you should not start a Twitter or a Facebook account just because everyone else is doing it, you shouldn't start a website without knowing your reasons for having it. Here is a solid foundation:

1 **Information.** To provide basic, 24/7 business information establishes credibility and contact information that anyone with an Internet connection can access.

2 **Sales.** Bottom line? Customers research the web before buying anything.

3 **Updates.** With a website that's under your control, you can update it as often as you want to. And with social media components, you can keep a live, real-time stream to allow you to update your information as frequently or infrequently as you choose.

4 **FAQs.** Answering frequently asked questions is an opportunity to show you know what you are talking about in detail; it is also a way to provide an information portal which customers and potential customers can use for research. This is a great way to enrich your customer service and cut down on unnecessary enquiries. This enables you to focus your responses to high-value customers.

5 **Cost.** Hosting your product and service catalog on the web is a lot cheaper than printing them over and over.

6 **Feedback.** It's an ideal hub for everything that your customers and partners have to say about you.

7 **Publicize specials.** Integrating this with email and social media promotions will give you another layer of relevance.

8 **Media.** Anytime a blogger, reporter, or researcher wants to find out about your company, they go to your website. That's where you can present the information you want them to find.

9 **Market research.** What better way to find out what your customers are thinking than to ask them on your website?

So you understand why you need one, but what do you need to get started, right?

WHAT YOU NEED

1   A domain name

There are a lot of options when you go to get a domain name. When considering what to choose, consider what you want people to find you as on the Internet. You can get a basic URL from a service like GoDaddy.com, and when you are shopping for a site name, there are a few things to keep in mind.

- **Simple.** Make sure that your domain name is your company name. If that name is taken and you can't purchase it from its current owner, consider the closest derivation of the name. Most domain name sellers will make recommendations.
- **.com.** While there are many other extensions (like .net, .org, .info, etc.), I highly recommend adjusting your domain name so that you can get a good .com URL. It is the most recognized domain extension, and most people will think of looking for yourname.com first, rather than yourname. Make it easy for them to find.

2   A designer

There is everything from free services that help you create a basic website in five minutes to expensive (and talented) web designers who will help you create something deeply customized.

- If you are part of a larger marketing department within a company, now is the time to start making proposals so that you can analyze your current website and get estimates on what it will take to get to where you want to be.
- If you are an individual affiliate marketer and just starting out, you may need to create your first website on your own. If that's the case,

I recommend utilizing one of the newer blog design themes through WordPress, like Thesis.

3 Site map

A site map is what will be included on your site, essentially a map of the pages and the content. Google "site map examples" to find some diagrams that will give you a good start. You'll need to customize these to what your goals and objectives are for your particular site.

4 Content

Research what other companies put on their websites and decide what you want to have on yours. You've read already that content is king, and here is where that maxim rings true, loud and clear. Unlike social media sites, your company website is where you are in control of all of the content. If your site is geared toward sales, creating a site that is full of content that leads your customers toward making a purchase is an art form in and of itself. If your site is geared more toward providing information for other companies or the media, you'll want to make sure that all of that information is easily accessible and frequently updated.

5 Usability

This is more of a design element than something tangible that you need, but it's important to think about this from the start. What do you want people to do on your site? Design the entire user experience around making it easy for users to understand your call to action and making that happen. What visitors see and how they navigate your site is the ultimate feedback on the success of your website in doing what you want it to do.

HOW TO USE IT IN PRACTICE

Now that you have a website with a solid structure, purpose, and it's been designed with usability in mind, it's time to make your website work for you. The most critical thing about a website is to keep it current with fresh content that reflects what is going on within your company.

HOW TO KEEP CURRENT

1   **Search Engine Optimization (SEO) and Search Engine Marketing (SEM).** This is how you help people find you and your website. For details, read the separate chapter on this aspect. I put it here to remind you that both SEO and SEM are ongoing processes that will need to be updated as you update other things on your site. Anytime you update the content that is on your website, you'll need to take a look at the basic and long-tail keywords you are focusing on and adjust accordingly.

2   **On the agenda.** Anytime there is a new marketing, advertising or sales update within the company, you need to make sure that the website adjusts accordingly. Don't let old taglines, out-of-date pictures and lapsed information hang out on your website because no one claims it as their responsibility. As of right now, it's your responsibility.

3   **Case studies.** If your company doesn't have case studies, start there. Go make some basic case studies that will print out as single page PDFs. Once you have those, make them readily accessible on your site – if not a tab on the homepage, then at least a featured spot on your "About" page.

4 **Social media links.** Depending on what kind of social media networks you've decided to become part of (at least Twitter and Facebook), you'll want to either feature feeds of those networks on your actual website or create homepage links to them. If you have the capability to show a live feed of your company's Twitter account, I highly recommend this as part of your homepage. If not the homepage of the website itself, then definitely the homepage of your blog.

5 **Newsletter.** While your website is the number 1 place for you to host your company messaging, you want people to ask you for more information. Make sure that there is a place for people to subscribe to your company newsletter, and store old copies of previous newsletters on your site as PDFs that people can download.

HOW TO MARKET YOUR WEBSITE

Because your website is the central hub for all information about your company, you'll want to make sure you market it properly. To do this, you have to get the name out there. Make sure your website is on all of the following.

1 **Business cards.** On your business cards and the business cards of every employee in your company. It's critical that people within your business start driving traffic toward your website. When you think about how to generate traffic, the first thing you realize is that you can't do it all alone – you need help. You need other people driving traffic to your website in order to make it successful. Sure,

getting customers and partners to do it will work, but start with the people who work for you already.

2   **Company literature.** Anything that your company prints needs to have the website address on it. Big and small, from quarterly reports and brochures to the posters you use at the conference. The more chances that people have to see where your website is, the more likely it is that they will visit.

3   **Video.** Your website should be listed at the end (or even the beginning) of every video that goes out as part of sales or marketing, or is posted on the Internet.

4   **Inbound links.** One of the first things to do to help get your website moving up the list on Google and other search engines is to get other people to link to you. It's good for your search engine ranking, good for being found in general, and it's good for general awareness, as the more places people see a link to your website, the more likely they are to visit.

5   **Social media listings.** Make sure that your company website is listed in the bio section of every social media network that you are part of. Volunteer it as an option to your employees if they themselves do not have a website and are looking for something to list when they sign up for social networking sites.

EXAMPLES

MARKETING WEBSITE: WWW.SETHGODIN.COM

Seth has a fantastic website that is simple, easy to understand, and directs you to a very specific call to action (see opposite).

Seth is a writer and he wants you to buy his books and read his blog. So they are both featured. There is a prominent link to his blog, and it's easy to see where to access his contact and speaking information.

It has the simplicity of an app with the information that lets you know everything you need to know about what he does. And it serves as a hub for all of his information, even as it makes clear calls to action to get you to go to other places.

ADVANCED USES

Once you have these basic elements in place on your website, it's time to start making it even more user-friendly, innovative and interactive. Here is where to start:

1   INCORPORATE YOUR BLOG

You don't have a blog yet? See my blogging chapter. And once you decide the who, what and how of your blog, make sure that it is a tab on the homepage of your website. For many users and researchers, this will be one of the first tabs they click on when they get to your site. Why? It's what you're up to right now, and it has the most human voice. While any company website is going to contain a lot of corporate speak and tailored messaging, blogging will always be a great way to offset that messaging with a human voice. And it will give people the most up-to-date information about what you and your company are up to within the branded context of your official website. Again, make sure it has its own tab on your homepage. Make it easy to find and, of course, keep it current.

2   INCORPORATE OTHER SOCIAL MEDIA

You've got the company Twitter feed and Facebook page linked, and that's a great start. But what other kinds of social media are you active in? If you have a Squidoo Lens (Squidoo is a website which ranks well in Google. Users can add pages called Lenses to the site) or brand page, how should you incorporate that? MySpace, YouTube, Google Buzz, LinkedIn and many other social networking links or feeds are a great way to extend what is going on with your website. Whether you use those networks enough to keep them current and interesting as links to your website is the real question – if no, don't incorporate them into your website. If yes, make sure they are featured.

3   INCORPORATE STAFF

While most people think about the product or service as the center-point of a good company or sales website, having a good staff page that introduces customers to who is behind the company is a great branding exercise. Often you'll see staff pages that are missing pictures or have interns up from three years ago ... if that's how it works for your company, it's better not to have it. But if you can get everyone in your office to submit a picture and OK a bio, go for it. Have fun with it – the point is to humanize the idea of your company.

WHAT THE FUTURE HOLDS

The Internet is dynamic by nature, especially with social media sites offering information in real-time from a variety of sources. Your employees, your customers, and everyone in your industry is creating information every day. The website you made last year may have great information and do a lot of things really well, but if you don't keep it updated and fresh, it won't be compelling enough to get people excited about what you are doing now.

Two trends I am seeing that websites are moving toward are becoming adaptable to the new ways that people are consuming content, like smartphones and tablets, and not just incorporating social media sites into their websites, but actually using those social media sites *as* their websites.

1   USER-FRIENDLY WEBSITES

People are buying smartphones. Millions of them. People are buying tablets. Millions of them. The traditional website doesn't work very well with these kinds of devices. Browsing the Internet on an iPhone or a Blackberry works, but it's cumbersome and is far from user-friendly. To get an idea of what websites will look like in the future, I think looking at the way app designers make their websites is incredibly instructive. Look at the difference between most websites and the website for TweetDeck (www.tweetdeck.com).

It's simple, it has large type, and it makes a few very simple points. This is the kind of design that comes from working with apps and smartphone graphics. Ease of use and lack of clutter is what they are all about, and that is where websites are going as they are being designed more and more for use by people on phones and tablets.

2   SOCIAL MEDIA AS A WEBSITE

Social media is a great way to represent your company to the world, and some Marketing agencies are choosing to take the ultimate step of letting their employees, clients and the Internet in general truly tell their story.

- **Modernista.** Modernista (opposite) is an advertising and branding agency that uses links to their social media pages in place of an about page. Notice the upper left corner, and the blog search that comes up for press in the background.
- **Campbell-Ewald.** Campbell-Ewald is one of the largest advertising and digital communications agencies in the US, and they have actually replaced their website with social media sites – all that remains is a branded sleeve along the left column. If you click on "the culture" under their "about us" section, you will be directed straight to their Facebook page.

I see these kind of radical (for now) integrations with social media becoming commonplace in corporate websites.

With websites struggling to become more interactive and things like Facebook pages struggling to become more business friendly, this is where the integration is going.

 TOOLS AND RESOURCES

1   HUBSPOT

Hubspot specializes in inbound marketing, which is essentially the science of making sure that people find *you* when they are looking for your company and your field online. They create software to create and grow your website traffic, generate leads and sales, and track everything around your campaign (www.hubspot.com).

2   WEBSITETIPS

There is a lot to keep up with when you are in charge of a website, from design aspects to strategies, to how to write the copy that represents your company online. This site has up-to-date information and an amazing archive of resources and tutorials that will keep you abreast of what you need to know as you need to know it (www.websitetips.com).

3   ANGELFIRE

For fun, this is a great site that shows and tells you exactly what should not happen on your website, just in case you forgot what websites used to look like ... www.angelfire.com/super/badwebs.

Chapter 4

Blogging

INTRODUCTION

You've heard the word a thousand times, and it probably seems like everyone and their brother has a "blog." The word's root is a mix of two words: "web" and "log." In the beginning, most blogs were just that – web logs of what people were doing, like personal journals. They then quickly evolved to become an important news channel, a network for thought leaders, and continue to grow in importance as the Internet presence of any business. Blogs give anyone the ability to publish, and blogging for business offers a number of communication opportunities.

Should you have one? The short answer is yes. Blogs are a key component of any Internet marketing campaign, and a valuable communication tool for any individual or business. They offer an authentic voice to communicate with your customers and potential leads. They also provide ongoing exposure for your company, product or service, and give you a way to be found through search engines. To me, a blog is as important to the Internet marketing of a company now as a website was five years ago. If you still only have a website, you're missing out on the real-time magic of the interactive web.

Starting a blog or keeping one going over time raises a number of questions for marketers. Who should write it? What do you write about? How do you manage employee disclosures?

In this chapter I'll look at how to set up a blog and address questions like who should write, what to write about, how to maintain and grow your blog, and what you can do to keep it vital and useful.

THE BASICS

When you decide to set up a blog (and I hope you've decided that by now) you'll want to consider two things before you start: audience and purpose.

AUDIENCE

Who are you talking to? Who do you want to read your blog?

I've seen marketers start a blog about their business and, on Monday, they write about what they can do for their customers, on Tuesday it's about what they offer other businesses in partnership, and on Wednesday it's about a summer holiday bonus for their employees. Writing for different audiences is a sure sign that a blogger hasn't thought about his or her readership. It's important to write to the same group of people for two reasons:

1   It narrows the range of topics and keeps you focused, and
2   It gives your readers a reason to come back.

Every other decision about creating and designing your blog, from the layout to the topics, will grow out of who you are talking to, and of course, what you are trying to do … which is next.

PURPOSE

What is the purpose of your blog? Think about this longer than you think about what color the background on your blog should be, and definitely longer than what the title of your blog should be. I see too many people get caught up in the design of their blog without a clear idea of who they are designing it for. Write about what your customers are going to be searching for. Write about common questions you have to answer.

If you choose to write to an audience of customers, are you trying to connect? Trying to inform them about new products? Trying to get feedback? Trying to highlight the stories of how they use your product?

If you choose to write to an audience of other businesses, are you trying to get their business? Are you trying to become an industry thought-leader? Are you trying to highlight the projects you do that go well?

There are as many purposes of a blog as there are blogs on the Internet. Whatever you choose is fine – there is no wrong choice. But whatever you choose, remember that the strength of a blog is in conversation – it is a communication tool, not a one-way broadcast of information.

The audience and purpose of my flagship blog, MurrayNewlands. com, have been critical in developing my strategy and fueling my growth. When I started my blog, I knew my audience was going to be the marketing community and my purpose was going to be building my network and providing people with ongoing exposure for their company, product or service. I also wanted to throw good information about online and social media marketing into the mix. I chose to focus a lot on interviews, new products and events in the marketing community for just those reasons, and my readers have become a great source of conversation.

HOW TO SET UP A BLOG

WORDPRESS VS BLOGGER

Once you decide to set up a blog, the first questions you'll have are: Where do I set it up? How do I do it?

The two biggest blog services are WordPress and Blogger, so I'll focus on them.

WordPress is an independent blog software. Blogger is a blog service created and hosted by Google. Both offer a free service, which is how many people start, so I am going to explain that here. I recommend going straight to setting up your own paid hosting (i.e. a service provider such as Hostgator which charges a monthly or annual fee) and using Wordpress. Here is a basic comparison of the free services.

Blogger

Blogger is a very simple, very basic blogger format. They have a three-step setup process.

1   Enter your basic information (email, password, etc.)
2   Name your blog.
3   Choose your template.

And after that, you've got a blog. Blogger blogs all contain the ".blogspot" element in their URL Internet address.

Blogger is a solid, easy to understand option for people who want a blog that is straightforward and easy to use.

WordPress

Setting up a WordPress.com blog is not difficult, as they show you on the WordPress.com homepage.

It's Easy As...

1   **Find a Web Host** and get great hosting while supporting WordPress at the same time.

2   **Download & Install WordPress** with our famous 5-minute installation.

3   **Consult the Documentation** and become a WordPress expert yourself.

If you want to know how to select a web host (service provider to host your blog), install WordPress and become a WordPress "expert," they'll show you how. But running that blog over the long-term is a complicated, involved process. And that's what I'll be discussing for the rest of this chapter.

WORDPRESS.COM VS WORDPRESS.ORG

The first thing to know is the difference between WordPress.com and WordPress.org.

- WordPress.com will set you up with a free blog that has a lot more bells and whistles than a Blogger blog. This blog will retain the WordPress name in the blog URL (i.e. www.exampleblogname. WordPress.com) and will not run all of the advanced options that WordPress makes available.

- WordPress.org will set you up with a blog that will work with your personal domain URL (e.g. www.murraynewlands.com), give you all of the powerful options that the WordPress format has to offer, and will give you the flexibility that I think every serious blogger needs.

Maybe I'm a little biased, but the bottom line for me is that if you're serious about blogging, you want a blog from WordPress.org. It will integrate with your personal or company's current URL, it will give you expanded and vital promotion and SEO options, and it will give you an email address that just displays *your* name, not the WordPress name.

Free is great, yes, but $10 a month is not going to kill your marketing budget, right? Trust me, it's worth it. www.godaddy.com is a great place to start.

HOW TO USE IT IN PRACTICE

CHOOSING YOUR THEME

Themes are blog templates. WordPress has hundreds of free "themes" available for you to choose from, and there are hundreds more with a variety of advanced capabilities that cost money. The great thing about a blogging software made specifically for bloggers is that you can be almost certain that someone before you has wanted a blog to look the way that you want it to.

WordPress.org will provide you with a list of the free theme options and a directory you can use to browse them. For the paid options, I recommend spending some time researching what theme offers the kind of advanced options that you want to utilize. I use the Thesis WordPress theme because of the powerful customization and SEO capabilities.

STEP BY STEP ON HOW TO WRITE A BASIC POST

Writing a post is as simple as typing a message and hitting publish, right? In some ways, yes – but, of course, if you want to do it right there is plenty more that goes into making it happen.

WordPress Dashboard basics

When you log in to your WordPress account, you'll see what's called the "Dashboard." It's your basic entry into everything that is going on behind the scenes of your blog. Pictured below is a snapshot of my blog's dashboard controls:

From left to right, the control options are: Posts, Media, Links, Pages, Comments, Appearance, Plugins, Users, Tools and Settings.

For the most part they are straightforward and do what they say they are going to do. Another popular layout for the same menu options is on the left vertical:

Menu options

- **Posts.** This is where you create a new post, edit or expand on a draft that you previously wrote and saved, or edit a post that you already published.

- **Media.** This is where all of the "media" that you add into your blog (pictures, videos, etc.) from anywhere else on the Internet is saved. You can also access or add to this library of media at any time when you are creating or editing your posts.

- **Links.** Similar to "Media," "Links" is a library of links you have used in your blog posts that you can access at any time.

- **Pages.** This is a menu of the different "Pages" inside your blog. All of your blog posts, your About Page, your Contact Page, and any other page you choose to create as part of your blog will be listed here.

- **Comments.** This is a library of all the comments that people have made on posts in your blog. They will wait here for you labeled as "Pending." You can choose to approve or delete them, or label them as spam.
- **Appearance.** In the beginning, you'll use this option a lot. It allows you to add and delete various elements to your blog page.
- **Plugins.** This option will give you access to all of the plugins available for your chosen WordPress theme. For more information, see the Plugins section later in this chapter.
- **Users.** This is a library of the different people who are "Users" or authors on your blog. If it's just you, you won't use this option much. If you are starting a blog that will have multiple contributors from your company, this is where you can see the activity divided by different authors of your blog.
- **Tools.** This option will give you access to additional tools available through WordPress.
- **Settings.** You'll want to go in once you first set up your WordPress blog and make sure the settings are filled out and adjusted the way you want them.

The best way to get familiar with how the WordPress layout works is to work with it. There is no substitute for just using the software for a few weeks. That said, here are a few basic guidelines to help you create your first post.

New post basics

My advice is to just start writing. I recommend writing your first post and getting it up there. I have seen too many people, marketers and others, agonize for weeks and even months over what their first post was going to be. Some of them never got around to actually starting their blog; it was over before it began and they were exhausted from thinking about it – with nothing to show.

Later in this chapter I've included ten ideas to help you get un-blocked, and if you're blocked before you even publish the first post, it's the ideal time to start using that list.

To write your first blog post:

1   Hover over the "Post" option at the top or side of the page and click on "Add New."

2   You'll see a screen that looks like this:

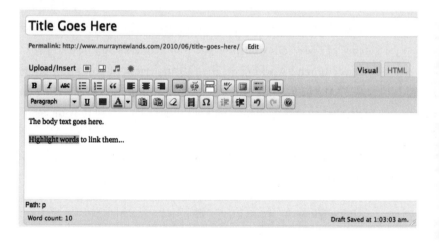

If you hover your mouse over the various buttons, you'll see a brief description of what each one does.

3   Type the title of your blog post into the top field where I have written "Title Goes Here." Just underneath this where it reads "Permalink: www.exampleblogname/titlegoeshere" your title will show up as part of the blog post URL. This is automatic and you don't have to do anything. If you want to change it, click on the

"Edit" button to the right of the URL and type in what you want
it to be.

4   Start typing your entry where I have typed "The body text goes
here." Many people like to type out their blog post in another text
program beforehand and copy/paste it into this field. This will
work but I don't recommend it – the formatting from a program
like Microsoft Word will affect how your text displays in Word-
Press. I recommend writing your posts in WordPress and saving
unfinished work as Drafts.

5   Visual vs. HTML. To the top right of the text field you will see
two tabs, "Visual" and "HTML." The "Visual" tab will display
your formatting the way it will appear on the blog post, whereas
the "HTML" tab will show the code. Unless you know HTML,
I recommend working on the "Visual" view. If you know some
HTML, or are just curious about learning it, you can click on
that tab and WordPress will automatically translate your visual
display into code.

6   Upload/Insert. Use these buttons to add visual media, like a
picture or a video, to your blog post.

Upload/Insert ▣ ▦ ♫ ✳

Each of these buttons will allow you to upload a different type of
media from your computer. To upload, I recommend first having
the media saved somewhere on your own computer.

The first box is for pictures, the second for movies, and the third for
music. The "star" button will upload many other kinds of media.

7   Adding Links. If you want to link some of the text inside your
blog post to another web page, first highlight the text you want to
link.

Then, go to the menu bar and click on the button that looks like a chain-link:

The button on the left will give you a screen where you can type or cut/paste in the URL you want to link to. If you later decide you don't want to link to that page anymore, highlight the text again and click on the right button and the link will disappear.

8   Categories. WordPress allows you to put your blog posts in categories.

These are some of the categories on my blog. As you can see, WordPress allows you to "+ Add New Category," which is what you'll need to do when you start out. I recommend adding two or three categories to start with and expanding later when you have more content.

To place your blog post in a category, click the box to the left of the category name. This will register when you publish your blog post and help organize your posts as you keep writing on your blog. It will also benefit the SEO of your articles.

9 Post Tags. WordPress is set up to help your blog posts get recognized and indexed by search engines. Post Tags are a good way to get your blog post to show up when people search for specific terms.

Inside the "Post Tags" field, type in words and terms that correspond to what you'd like your blog post to show up as when people type a search term into Google. For example, if this chapter were a blog post, I may tag my post with "WordPress," "WordPress Instructions," and "WordPress Intro."

You can click "Add" after each new Post Tag, or you can type in multiple Post Tags at once, separated by commas and click add for all of them at once. (For example: WordPress, WordPress Instructions, WordPress Intro)

10 Publishing. When you are satisfied with your blog post, it's time to take the plunge and publish. For this, there is a very basic box at the top right of the page:

If you want to save a draft of your post to come back to later, click "Save Draft." If someone else needs to read through your post before it is published, you can click on the "Edit" link next to Status: Draft, and the dropdown will allow you to save your draft as "Pending," which is a separate label for a draft that is ready to go but waiting for review.

If you are ready to publish right now, click the large blue "Publish" button.

If you are ready to publish but want to schedule your post to publish at a later time, click on the "Edit" link next to Publish immediately. This will take you to a calendar where you can specify the day and time that you'd like to have your blog post published.

ONCE YOU START WRITING, THESE TWO THINGS WILL HAPPEN

There are two things that happen to every blogger I know at some point.

1   You slack off

Everyone starts out with their schedule, whether it's planning to write every day or once a week. And most people do well for a few weeks, but by the end of the first month, they've already cheated a little here and written shorter posts, or a little there and posted a day late. When you are your own boss or the first to create a blog at your company, chances are nobody is looking over your shoulder.

It's going to happen – the key is to not let it happen more than once. If you skip a post on your schedule, don't try to make up for it with two the next time. I call this your blogger margin of error. You're allowed to miss, but start up again and get back on schedule. If you had planned to post every day and you miss a Tuesday, post again Wednesday. Then Thursday. Then Friday. If you're weekly, the same concept applies.

2   You (think you) run out of ideas

Expect to start out with a lot of ideas. Then, a month later, expect to feel like you have nothing left to write about. Expect to think it often as you keep blogging. I guarantee it will never be true. When you think you've run out of ideas, this is the time when your blog is ready to grow – it's actually an opportunity. You have the chance to expand what your blog is and what it is about. When you hit a run of writer's block, here are ten ideas to get you writing again:

1   **Current events.** Write about something happening that relates to your industry.
2   **Debate.** Find a post by someone else in your industry that you don't agree with or think you have a better perspective on. Write a blog post and send it to them, get them to comment. It's a great way to energize your writing.

3   **Revisit.** Find an old post that got some traffic or people responded to. Go back and revise it, then promote it again. If it got traffic the first time, it will get it again.

4   **Keywords.** Go to www.google.com/trends/hottrends and there will be a list of the "most searched for" keywords for the day. Write a post that connects one of those keywords to your industry (Hint: Make sure to put the keyword in your title – you'll get some extra traffic!)

5   **Interviews.** It doesn't have to be all about you – in fact, it shouldn't be. Interview someone and post that on the blog – a customer, a client, someone else in your business.

6   **Solve a problem.** Every field has problems that people experience. Write about how you have solved one of those problems – as a bonus, a post like this has a good chance of getting passed along.

7   **Highlight others.** Write a post highlighting the best bloggers in your industry. Chances are they monitor the web, so you'll get feedback and comments from them. It also gives you a good excuse to email them with a link to your blog.

8   **Polls and contests.** Start a poll or contest through your blog. Again, this will get you traffic and give people a reason to pass your blog along.

9   **Guest bloggers.** Invite other bloggers to write on your blog. Hopefully, they'll do the same for you.

10   **Top 10 lists.** Top 10 lists generate traffic. Make a top ten list about the best, worst, craziest, strangest, newest, etc. in your field … you'll be amazed how fast you fill up the page.

Those are just ten ideas. If you use these up and get stuck again, write a blog post about ten new ways to get past writer's block – you'll be amazed at how creative you can get.

 **EXAMPLES**

CHRIS BROGAN (WWW.CHRISBROGAN.COM)

Chris Brogan is one of the more successful bloggers on the Internet. He focuses on humanizing business through blogging, and the two things that I think make his blog an excellent example of what a blog can be are his focus on 1) giving away advice and content and 2) interacting with his readers.

1   He gives away advice and guidance daily, and it's often from things that he is trying that are on the cutting edge. You learn something when you read his blog.

2   He responds to comments on his blog when people make them. And he responds to people on Twitter – both with an intensity that is tough to maintain. But it's why he's good. Imagine if you commented on the work of someone famous in your neck of the woods – and then they responded to you! Would you be back to read again? Absolutely.

He does the basics consistently and authentically: Give away content. Respond when people comment.

You can learn a lot from those simple suggestions.

THE HUFFINGTON POST (WWW.HUFFINGTONPOST.COM)

The Huffington Post does a better job than any other blog I know of in writing headlines, and that's why I have it in this section. There are a handful of good tips about headline writing – use numbers or celebrities, make lists, and ask questions – but the Huffington Post has it all down to a science. And they know how to pick a picture.

You read a marketing blog and more often than not the image will be something from a clip art library or, worse yet, a logo from a conference. If you want to get an idea of what people like to look at for pure sugary-attractiveness, browse the Huffington Post homepage every week or two. You'll pick up on their tactics for writing headlines that make you want to read and how they use pictures that draw you in. Just don't get lost there and forget to write your own blogpost!

ADVANCED USES

Successful blogs become the focus of communities and enable market leadership and sometimes market domination. Blogging as the heart of a conversation of a community will develop beyond the blog into other media and real-life events. The well-known blog Mashable has large communities on Facebook, Twitter, LinkedIn as well as real-life meetings around the world. Mashable.com also has events and event award shows.

A good example of this is the outreach achieved by Gary Vaynerchuk with his blog about wine. He is now held in high regard as a world leading expert on wine and sells millions of dollars of wine every year through his blogs. He also speaks internationally about wine as well as having several bestselling books. He has celebrity status both online and in real life.

Chris Brogan (www.chrisbrogan.com) became well known through his blog and now has a career as a public speaker as well as having his own conferences. He too has number of bestselling books.

WHAT THE FUTURE HOLDS

Blogging will continue to evolve and change. Ten years ago it was something that people were just starting to use to keep online journals. Five years ago it was still something most businesses had never heard of.

There are several big influences on blogging in the future.

1   MOBILE

In the last two years there has been an explosion in mobile devices, and they will change the future of blogging in a few important ways. The first way will be formatting. As the use of "smart" mobile devices grows, it will become increasingly important for blogs to publish in a format (theme) that can easily translate to a smartphone format, or be turned into an app with relative ease.

On the other side of the same issue, it will become more and more common to see people live-blogging events as they happen from smartphones while those events are still going on. For example, with an iPhone or an Android device, a journalist can take pictures, video, and statements from politicians or sports teams during an event and put it all together in a blog post, complete with commentary. They can post it from their phone before they even leave the stands.

2   TABLET

Blogs integrate text, video and podcasting. That's pretty much exactly what the new group of tablets (the iPad and beyond) will deliver, but they'll do it with a more interactive ability than any device or format we've ever seen in the past. Blogs will adapt to this new delivery device as they have to for every other shift in online media.

Some of the big advantages will be integrating video with posts in a more streamlined way, or allowing for posts to read like books, similar to the way ebook readers like the Kindle allow for now.

3 YOUTH

Just about every college graduate is coming out of school with an understanding of what blogging is and how it relates to business. They are up on the technology and could very well have their own blog. If you are going to hang on to your job as a marketer, you'll need to be able to create and facilitate a blog, but you'll also have to figure out how to communicate with people who are integrating social networks and blogs into their everyday lives, not to mention smartphones and tablets.

4 NEW LAYOUTS

Advanced theme setups like "Thesis" and "Headway" are making it easier and easier for bloggers who don't know anything about code to make dynamic and impressive blogs that integrate with the rest of their websites. Thesis will continue to improve as a WordPress theme and get even better at optimizing blogs for search engines, and Headway is starting to make it possible for people who don't know code to take real visual control of their blogs, which will make the future a whole lot more interesting, especially when you consider the evolving tablet market.

TOOLS AND RESOURCES

1   LORELLE ON WORDPRESS (WWW.LORELLE. WORDPRESS.COM)

Lorelle VanFossen is a true WordPress aficionado. Her blog reflects that kind of love and is packed with eight years worth of information, commentary and discussion around everything you want to know about blogging on WordPress. She gets very technical about every aspect, and has a palpable love for the community of people who use WordPress.

2   WEBINKNOW (WWW.WEBINKNOW.COM)

This blog from marketing and leadership strategist David Meerman Scott is a good resource for staying on top of the online marketing trends from the larger, strategic view. He deals a lot with strategy and macro-trends.

3   PROBLOGGER (WWW.PROBLOGGER.NET)

Darren Rowse is a highly successful blogger who writes an excellent blog about blogging. He will get into the nitty-gritty about how to do specifics on blogs, tips and how-to's for the day-to-day blogging, and hosts probably the best blogger job board on the web.

4   THE BUSINESS OF BLOGGING AND NEW MEDIA (WWW.CHRISG.COM)

Bottom line, Chris Garrett just always has great posts that are to the point and helpful. He's a blogging and Internet marketing consultant who writes as honestly and openly as I feel like he would talk to me if we were sitting in the pub.

5 COPYBLOGGER (WWW.COPYBLOGGER.COM)

This is a blog about blogging by bloggers who love it. Subtitled "copy-writing tips for online marketing success," this is the kind of blog you go to when you need to get out of a rut, find some inspiration and feel like you're not the only one who stares at the blank page and wonders what to write about …

6 MURRAYNEWLANDS.COM

My blog is all about connection – I'd love to see you there. I focus on interviewing people in the industry and letting my readers know about what's new in the online marketing space. Want to do an interview or have an event to promote? Visit my blog and let me know about it.

Chapter 5

Online PR and Blogger Outreach

INTRODUCTION

Just as traditional PR is focused on creating and maintaining the public image of a company and communicating with the general public, online PR is concerned with doing these things but through the Internet. Broadly defined, online public relations involves everything from blogger and social media outreach to search engine optimization and brand reputation monitoring.

Many traditional PR firms and departments are shifting large parts of their efforts toward online PR, and for the simple reason that the public is online, you need to be involved. Press releases are now old hat.

BLOGGER OUTREACH AS PUBLIC RELATIONS

Blogging is a marketing force that influences public opinion, creates powerful business relationships, and plays an important role in building an online brand. As people spend more and more time online, blogs have taken on a more influential role, and people turn to them for information and opinion. Creating and maintaining relationships with influential bloggers in your field is critical to the success of any online product launch or ongoing outreach.

SOCIAL MEDIA AS PUBLIC RELATIONS

Social media networks allow people to talk with their friends, family and, increasingly, companies and brands. Because social media have created multiple channels where people can speak directly to brands and companies and the conversations are innately public, social media have quickly become an important part of any online public relations strategy. If you want to relate to the public, you need to be interacting with them where they are. In addition, any blogger you want to reach as part of an outreach campaign is on some form of social media, probably Twitter. Cultivating and maintaining a legitimate presence over time will make outreach easier when you need it.

SEARCH ENGINE OPTIMIZATION AS PUBLIC RELATIONS

Making sure that your company appears high on search engine results is important for presenting the information you want people to see when they are looking for businesses in your field. Because most people will do a basic Internet search and then use results on the first page, you want your website and articles you like to be on that page.

BRAND MONITORING AS PUBLIC RELATIONS

Knowing where conversations are happening on the web about your company allows you to gauge public opinion and reaction, and it allows your company to join those conversations. Because of the nature of the real-time web, knowing about those conversations as they are happening enables you to join in. This kind of real-time interaction can go a long way toward helping you deal with situations as they arise, not the next day when they are in the headlines.

In this chapter I will focus on how to approach successful blogger outreach, and touch on how social media, search engine optimization and brand monitoring factor into overall online PR.

THE BASICS

BLOGGER OUTREACH

Blogs are a powerful new communication avenue, and in many ways are becoming as important and trusted as major newspapers and magazines. Many people come to trust the articles and opinions of bloggers through the relationships they form with them, and in order to be successful in your own blogger outreach, that's exactly what you need to do: form relationships with bloggers.

At the core, blogs are about conversation and interaction, and they are written by people with a real passion for their subject matter. Keep in mind that most of the people you will be reaching out to build their blogs from the ground up, and that they started writing because they loved their topic, not because someone was paying them to write.

Why you need blogger outreach as part of your PR strategy

- Blogging adds a human component to an increasing digital and technological age.
- People trust other people more than a brand's own messaging, and blogging gives brands a face (Nielsen Global Online Consumer Survey 2009).
- Blog coverage increases your product sales.
- Contributing to established blogs enables you to have a voice in industry publications through guest blogging.

SOCIAL MEDIA

Social media as a public relations channel is a no brainer. The people who are heavy social media users like to talk, they like to interact. Your job is to be where they are and interact with them. This is important because it's a chance for a company to talk to people on a personal and real-time level. Understanding that word of mouth through social media spreads a message, good or bad, as fast as any other media channel means understanding that you need to have a presence where it counts. When people hear something about your company or product through social media, you need to have an account there to become part of the conversation to either verify or dispel.

SEARCH ENGINE OPTIMIZATION

Optimizing search results is also key to maintaining a positive online presence. While I have written a separate chapter on how to do SEO, there are some specific and compelling reasons for making it part of both your sales strategy *and* your online PR approach.

1   **Journalists use search engines.** If you want to get a message out, you'll want to have your message where the journalists are looking.
2   **Credibility.** Making sure the right messaging shows up in search engine results will help anyone, from journalists to the general public, verify and trust what you are saying about yourself.
3   **Speaking to consumers.** If you can place your own messaging in search engine results, the chances of consumers finding them when they need them are much higher than finding it in a traditional print publication.

BRAND MONITORING

There are two main reasons you want to monitor your brand online:

1 **Real Time.** You can take part in conversations where they are happening, when they are happening. Brand monitoring software will give you periodic updates of every mention of your brand or company across the blogosphere, major news outlets, social media and forums. When you find one that you want to be a part of, you can go there and join in.

2 **Reputation.** So that you can get the jump on any kind of negative press that your company is getting online. In the same way, you can go and be part of negative conversations going on about your brand. If it's a blog post or a series of blog posts coming out after a major product launch, for example, you'll be able to get in on the commenting right after the post is published. Alternately, you will be able to contact the blogger or write your own post addressing the same issues.

 HOW TO USE IT IN PRACTICE

BLOGGER OUTREACH

Whether it's a product launch, publicity pitch or brand management, reaching out to, meeting, and maintaining good relations with bloggers in your field is a critical way to communicate online. I'm going to focus on blogger outreach around a new product or event.

As with any platform there are "rules of engagement." It is important to do your research and only contact bloggers who actively write about your industry – the more specific the better. Taking a blanket approach will not get you the exposure or engagement you are looking for. How you pitch to a blogger is important. Making contact with a blogger should not sound like a sales pitch and the information should not be sent in the form of a formal press release.

Build relationships now

Start building relationships with bloggers in your field that you think you'll want to pitch in the future *before* you are pitching anything. Establishing and maintaining relationships will help to avoid the eleventh hour deadline, and it may even get you involved in some articles or projects through those blogs you wouldn't have known about otherwise. We've all had the friend or business associate who we only hear from when he/she needs something – if you wait until you need a blogger to write about you to introduce yourself, you're that guy.

Blogger outreach should ideally be an ongoing process of leaving feedback and comments, of interacting and participating on blogs. The advantage to you is that a blogger will recognize your name when you need him/her, and you aren't having to start the relationship from scratch. If you establish a good relationship with a blogger and he/she likes what you do, he/she may even help you come up with ideas about how to build a better brand presence online.

Who to pitch?

Bloggers write about what they are passionate about, and you should know what that is. You want to find people who write about what you do. You don't want to pitch bloggers who don't write about something related to your business or product – there needs to be a point of connection. Start by reading some of their recent posts and their "About" page. Knowing what they like and have been writing about lately will help when you approach them.

Working with A-list bloggers is great for exposure, but many of them are already associated with a brand, or don't want to associate with brands at all. Working with mid-tier niche bloggers who have a consistent audience can be a great move for a few reasons. Chances are they don't get as many pitches, so your attention will stand out. And if they have a good track record of writing and a solid audience, you know that they have readers who respect their opinion, and probably other bloggers who read their posts. Another advantage of mid-tier bloggers is that they can be easier to please and can often work to tighter deadlines. Also, all bloggers started somewhere, and today's mid-tier blogger could be tomorrow's A-lister.

In the end, pitch bloggers in your field who have an audience, whether they are A-listers or mid-tier. Every post helps, and your goal should be to build relationships.

Tone

The best way to contact a blogger is as if you were approaching an acquaintance of a mutual friend. Remember that the blogosphere is conversational, so I recommend avoiding obvious pitches, the press release synopsis and the canned stories. Be friendly and not too corporate, but keep it professional – you don't know them yet, and they don't know you.

How to contact bloggers

1   **Email.** The most effective way to contact a blogger is through the email that he/she lists on their site. Alternately, they may have a contact form as part of their blog. If they list contact information, that is how they want to be contacted.

2   **Guest posts.** If you or your business has a blog, you can also ask to guest post on relevant blogs as part of your blogger outreach. In

kind, you can ask bloggers you want to work with to write for your blog.

3   **Find them online.** Bloggers don't just live online on their blog, of course. Many of them are extremely active on social media, so looking for bloggers through Twitter, Facebook or LinkedIn is a great way to find them. Also, looking on HARO, Business-2Blogger, Bloggerlinkup.com, Juta 42 or Mashable are great resources.

4   **Off-line blogger scouts.** Another way to approach bloggers is off-line. You can invite bloggers into your environment. They are real people and have to leave the house sometime. They are often looking for stories, so if you have one to tell, they'll listen. A good example is inviting bloggers to trade shows. Invite them in so that you can give them information on your brands and allow them the opportunity to interview you in person. Venues like the London Blog Club or the Cyber Mommy Meet-up in London are great examples of off-line blogger contact.

MAKING YOUR PITCH

Keep it real

Your first interaction should be personal and real. It doesn't have to be long and it shouldn't be full of you asking the blogger to write about your product or business. You should make it clear that you know what the blogger is about and how you are related, tell them how you can add value to what they are doing, and provide a link where they can learn more about you.

Don't send a press release to a blogger. Don't send a mass email to dozens of people at the same time. Don't send attachments.

Bloggers have egos

Like anyone, bloggers have egos, and they like it when you speak to that ego. Rather than pitching something as "appealing to your readers," pitch it as something you want to give to them because they are a respected voice in the space. And when you are interacting with them, that communication should come from your marketing director, not from an intern.

Also, bloggers can smell marketing jargon and sales pitches before the email even gets to their inbox. Don't bother with it.

Be clear

When you are working with a blogger, be clear and transparent about the offering and the expectations. The blogging community is small and bloggers talk to each other. Be clear and consistent with what you offer and what your expectations are.

Respond quickly

If bloggers are responding to your pitches, that's great news! Remember to maintain a strong sense of professionalism and respond quickly to answer questions or send additional information. Bloggers are on-line all the time and they are used to going back and forth several times in a day and working quickly with content.

What bloggers want

At some point, everyone is going to ask, "What's in it for me?" Bloggers understand that they have power and influence with their readers, and should they chose to endorse a product, they are going to be selective about it.

Even if you aren't paying a blogger to write a post, offering exclusivity, first reviews, private viewings, unique offerings, special VIP status, coupons, special discount codes and allocation of invites to exclusive events or exclusive reader options are all great ways to compensate a blogger.

If you or your company have a blog, another great way to build a relationship with them and say thank you is to provide links to their content. If they have already written about something related to what you do, link to their posts. If they do write about your company or product, link to their post on your press page.

Know what you're doing

Bloggers are like anyone else – they say what they think. If you have a good product or service, bloggers will say so. Bloggers will research your product and find out the good, bad and ugly before they are going to make an association with your brand.

When doing blogger outreach, make sure that they are as excited about your brand as you are. The relationship should be one of mutual gain not one where you have to talk them into writing about you.

AFTER THE POST

Follow up

Absolutely follow up with every blogger who wrote a post. I even recommend following up with those who you exchanged emails with whether they wrote a post or not. If they see others writing about you, they may be more inclined to write something later, or next time you are doing an outreach.

Publicize

If a blogger writes a post about your product or business, do everything you can to publicize that post. Push it out through your social media networks, add it to your press page, and quote it in your next newsletter.

Keep it going

If a blogger wrote about your product or business, keep that relationship going after the post. Keep them up to date with other products, free trials and discounts. You could even give them the ability to test products for you depending on what industry you are in. This could add buzz for your product and their blogging site and the interaction could start all over again.

To establish a long-term relationship with a blogger, find out what their goals are, how you can help them, and if there is a possibility for you to work together on future projects.

SOCIAL MEDIA

Bloggers spend time on social media. Real people spend time on social media. You're spending time on social media. Where else do you frequently find writers, marketers and real people all in the same place? Utilizing social media specifically for public relations shines in a few instances:

1 **Product launches.** You know that people will be talking about your company when a new product comes out, so you want to be ready to be part of those conversations. Using social media in tandem with a good brand monitoring tool is ideal for staying on top of what people are saying, reacting to it, or pointing people in the right direction for the right information.

2 **Twitter chats.** Whether it's with a blogger, a customer, or just someone curious, talking to people through social media has a ripple PR effect. How you treat that one person and the

information you give them will reverberate throughout that social media network.

SEARCH ENGINE OPTIMIZATION

Using SEO as a PR tool differs slightly from using it purely as a way to get your content to appear high in the search rankings.

1   **Keywords.** Your keyword choices and focuses are different than they would be for sales. For public relations purposes, consider optimizing a page on your company website specifically for breaking news on your company, and using that page as your press hub. That way when people search for "Your Company Press Release" or something like that, they will find a resource page that you can update as you wish.

2   **Press releases.** While press releases are old hat for getting the word out, they can be good for SEO. When you have something big going on for your company, the press (online or print) will be looking for information about it. You want your press release to be one of the things they find when they do a search. If you are the person responsible for making this happen, I recommend that you look into a press release service like PRWeb. Using free press release sites can get you some results, but they are largely unreliable for really getting your release the kind of page-one exposure you want, and the results are often spotty. In the end, you get what you pay for. You can only get so many pages from the same domain name to appear on a search result page, so hosting it on a service like PRWeb will also give you the chance of having even more results when journalists and potential customers are researching your launch.

BRAND MONITORING

Brand monitoring is important and Google Alerts is a great place to start. Who could ever monitor every social media network and blog? There are, however, a wide variety of options ranging from free to thousands of dollars per month that can give you an idea of what is going on around the web.

FREE OPTIONS

If you are just starting out, you may want to get your feet wet by seeing what kind of results you can get from using the free options that are out there. The first of these is your network within your company – make it known that you are the hub for any information that people find on the Internet about your company, and ask that they send you links to articles they read.

1   **Google Alerts.** This service is free and does a great job of sending you blog and news articles that mention your company name or other chosen keywords. You can have them sent to your email inbox.
2   **Technorati.** It's a blog search engine, and everyone is registered. They will monitor any links to your blog and let you know about them.
3   **Backtype.** This service will monitor blog comments across the web for mentions of your company or other keywords.
4   **Boardtracker.com.** This is a discussion board and forum search engine.

5   **Social Mention.** This is a social media search engine that will give you an idea of where your company name is popping up across social networking sites.

ADVANCED USES

BLOGGER OUTREACH

The basic blogger outreach strategy is figuring out who you should be talking to, establishing a relationship with them, and maintaining that relationship. Anything you can do to take that relationship off-line is an advanced "use" in my book. If you are having any kind of a social event, product launch, or other celebratory event, invite bloggers you have a relationship with. Better yet, sponsor the local blogger meetup to get your name out there as a company that is supportive of bloggers in general.

SOCIAL MEDIA

Maintaining your social media accounts is a challenge, but well worth the time and effort with the rewards you can get through online PR. Taking your social media presence beyond listening and reacting to actively seeking out like-minded consumers or B2B relationships and starting conversations is the ideal way to step up your social media game and get yourself known not just as a participant, but as a thought leader.

SEARCH ENGINE OPTIMIZATION

If you already have the web pages and news about your company on page one of Google, it's time to start thinking about where people go once they get to those pages. What do you want them to do next? Sign up for a newsletter? Set up a sales call? Buy something on the website? Look at what is the most prominent call to action on your high-ranking pages and make sure you are setting the user up to go where you want them to go.

BRAND MONITORING

Keeping tabs on what people are saying about your company is important, and engaging in conversations is even more so. The best and most advanced way to use brand monitoring is to compare the amount and value of the conversations that happen before, during and after a product launch, blogger outreach campaign, or other online PR venture. Conversation ebb and flow in the online world can tell you a lot about what to expect elsewhere and help you stay on top of your response game overall.

 WHAT THE FUTURE HOLDS

BLOGGER OUTREACH

As blogging becomes more and more accepted as an influential form of new media, the reach and power of bloggers will continue to grow. I expect to see some codification of how blogger outreach happens, but never a complete move away from the personal aspect. Instead I expect print publication interactions to begin basing themselves on what is happening in the blog world. In addition, I expect a much wider adoption of the social media or multimedia press release as publications begin to think of their online publications as more and more important.

SOCIAL MEDIA

Social media will continue to grow and become even more enmeshed in daily life. With the addition of location-based services to the roster of mainstream services, the way that sources for stories are networked to bloggers and other online journalists will become even more local and real-time based.

SEARCH ENGINE OPTIMIZATION

Every site or page can benefit from link-building and, as Google and other search engines change their algorithms, the one indicator that will remain strong is to be referenced by other people on the Internet. By having strategic links in the press releases that you distribute and promote back to pages on your website you can increase their standing in search engine results.

BRAND MONITORING

One of the hardest things to do with Internet-wide brand monitoring is truly measure the sentiment of what's being said. With all of the ways that different words can be used, it can be difficult to determine whether a mention of your company is good or bad. But the practice of understanding the context is improving, and I see that as being one of the big places for innovation in the coming years. Right now I see

PeopleBrowsr (www.peoplebrowsr.com/) doing the best job with this and leading the way.

TOOLS AND RESOURCES

BLOGGER OUTREACH

1   **Meetups.** Get to know the blogger meetups that happen in your city and start attending. Even if you are there as a beginning blogger for your own company's website, being a recognizable face in that community is important.

2   **Niche Forums.** Do an Internet search for the niche forums and chat rooms in your field or industry. That's where the highest concentration of the bloggers who are on the cutting edge and love to talk about it will be.

3   **Your own network.** This sounds silly at first, but if you are in marketing, you know a lot of bloggers within one to two degrees of separation. Cast your net both over the Internet and out to your trusted colleagues and my guess is that, in no time, you'll have a list much longer than you expected.

SOCIAL MEDIA

1   **Brian Solis:** www.briansolis.com. Brian Solis is generally acknowledged to be at the cutting edge of writing in online PR. Solis has helped to shape the influence of emerging media and its conversions of marketing communications and publishing. He is a digital analyst, sociologist, and even a futurist.

　　You want to read what he has to say about online and PR.

2 **Mashable:** www.mashable.com. Mashable is the best resource for what's new with social media, and bloggers keep up with that kind of thing – keeping up with it yourself by scanning their headlines or reading their weekly top ten article recaps will help keep you in the know.

SEARCH ENGINE OPTIMIZATION

1 **SEOMoz** (www.seomoz.org). This website has a slew of great tools to help you work on your SEO yourself.

2 **PRWeb** (www.prweb.com). This paid service will optimize your press release for search engines.

3 **Lee Odden's Top Rank Blog** (www.toprankblog.com/category/seo). The SEO section of Lee's blog is a great resource for how SEO and online PR fit together.

BRAND MONITORING

1 PeopleBrowsr (www.peoplebrowsr.com). This service does a great job of data mining, analytics and brand engagement.

Chapter 6

Video Marketing

INTRODUCTION

As a marketer, you want to be where the eyeballs are, and those eyeballs are increasingly turning to online video in one form or another. But whether you're targeting YouTube, Blip.tv, Vimeo, Hulu, or somewhere else, it's important to acknowledge that the list is huge and keeps on growing. According to YouTube's own fact sheet,

> "People are watching 2 billion videos a day on YouTube and uploading hundreds of thousands of videos daily. In fact, every minute, 24 hours of video is uploaded to YouTube."

And as the Videonuze noted last summer, online video viewing during traditional prime-time television hours is up to over 62 million viewers in the US. Nothing to sneeze at, and a sure indication that people are watching online video during their leisure time. Add that to the consistently growing daytime viewing numbers.

Of course, "online video" is a broad category. There are different ways to use video, and how you choose to go about it has a lot to do with what your goals are and what you are trying to accomplish. What people tend to think of first when they think of online video is viral videos. This can be a great guerrilla marketing strategy, if building buzz for something new is what you want to do.

But not everyone needs a viral video. If you have a site with specific products, using video to show that product in action will give your potential customers a much better idea of what you're selling. If you are promoting an event or a group, video is a phenomenal way to introduce your audience to the people involved in your event. If you have a blog, creating a short welcome video gives your readers a chance to identify with you beyond your words alone. And finally, if you are willing to take the social media plunge with video, actively starting video blogging (Vlogging) conversations through YouTube or soliciting community videos through a Facebook Fan Page can be a powerful way to get your customer base involved.

Creating and uploading video to any of the online sites is inexpensive (usually free) and simple to do. But the bottom line? Online video is one of the easiest ways to make a personal connection.

 THE BASICS

To use video in any online marketing venture, you need three things:

1   video hardware,
2   video software, and
3   strategy.

You don't need to be an expert at production or editing – in fact, if you have an Apple computer, you can learn how to use a program like iMovie in just a few hours.

ON YOUR BLOG

This is where I think video has the best reach. Because a blog is all about conversation and creating your brand image, what better way to diversify your approach than to utilize the power of video? You can include a welcome video on your homepage, embed videos or talks that you like in your blog posts, or invite users to contribute videos as part of a larger project. Whatever you do, the power, I believe, is in the personalizing. We all feel connected to faces we can see and voices we can hear, and that can only be good for your brand.

OUTSIDE THE OFFICE

Video is an easy way to conduct interviews, record speakers or sessions you like, or even give your co-workers a tour of the conference you are attending. To make it happen, all you need is a smartphone and a You-Tube channel. If you're going to be recording video, I recommend testing your battery life and knowing when and where to recharge – the last thing you want is to be at a conference when your phone isn't working!

IN YOUR MARKETING

Video adds a visual to your marketing copy voice, but it's important to think of it as different from a commercial. Whether you are creating a (hopefully) viral video, branded content, or something more like a "how-to" or "behind the scenes" video, the most powerful thing video will do for you is define your brand. It's important how good the quality is, the editing, and that the message is clear. Think about the kinds of videos you watch and think "hmmm, that was good ..." and start there. Create something of value for your customers and they will share it with each other.

 HOW TO USE IT IN PRACTICE

Making and uploading video has become easy and inexpensive, yet many marketers continue to treat it as "something that other people are doing ..." I think you should use it. It's versatile, accessible, and the fact that it inherently promotes a personal connection means it is part of the human side of marketing that I believe is so important.

But first thing's first – you have to know how to get your movie ready to share.

TO START PUTTING VIDEOS ON YOUTUBE

- **Create.** Use iMovie and save it as .mp4 or .mov (.mp4 and .mov are popular types of video format which are compatible with YouTube and many other video sharing websites to which you will want to upload your videos).
- **Upload.** Uploading a video to YouTube is your first step. They make it very easy for people to send the link, embed the video in their blog or web page, and people are comfortable with the YouTube interface. Use it. There is a fun tutorial from "The Ant Farm" about how to upload your video here: www.youtube.com/watch?v=SzSwnbxb9TY.

A few key things to keep in mind:

1   **User account.** When you create your user account, choose a name that is general enough to upload all of your future videos to. If you have a blog already, that's a great name to choose. Alternately, if the name of your company is still available, that is ideal.
2   **Title.** Choose a title that contains one or more of the keywords you've chosen to work with for your SEO. Make sure it is something that people search for.
3   **Description.** Keep this short, and use keywords again.
4   **Tags.** List out all of your keywords and relevant terms for this video.

5   **Link.** Make sure you link from your YouTube description to your
website.

ON YOUR BLOG

- **Introduction.** If you have a blog, welcome people with a video. This
doesn't need to be long and it doesn't need to be over-rehearsed.
Make a 30-second video in which you greet people, introduce
yourself, and tell them what your blog is all about.
- **Interaction.** Creating a YouTube channel and becoming an active
Vlogger as part of your blogging activities has many rewards. First,
you connect with a group of people who are technologically inclined
and probably big sharing voices on the Internet – if they like your
company, that's a good thing. Second, you immediately have people
to ask for help if you are still learning the ins and outs of video.
Third, there's a different dynamic to interacting over video than
there is to the typed comments on a blog – that keeps you thinking
and keeps your content fresh.
- **Inspiration.** You don't always have to be the one creating the video.
Embedding video that you find inspiring is a great way to share
something with your customer base, inspire them, and then connect it back to your company. Including a fun or inspiring video in
your blog post sets it apart – you show *and* tell at the same time.

OUTSIDE THE OFFICE

- **Interview.** One of the greatest ways to showcase the people you
admire and respect is to interview them for your blog – and, as an
added bonus, those people will probably write about or send traffic
to that video or blogpost. You can use video as a great reason to

spend time talking with people, learn from them, and share that learning with the world.

- **How-to's.** If you have a product or service that needs any kind of "how-to," video is the ideal tool to help people understand what's hard to put into words. How-to videos for anything that has complicated instructions allows people to watch someone else putting a product together; they can rewind, pause, and take the instructions at their own pace. Or, if your product is a digital one, a screencast will allow you to show and walk someone through the set-up or troubleshooting process, which is always more illuminating than writing it out. Show instead of telling.

IN YOUR MARKETING

The advantage of using video in your marketing is that it speaks to people where they already are. Notice that I say you can use video in your marketing, not in your advertising. If you want to buy ad space in between Hulu programs or ads that pop up at the bottom of YouTube videos, go for it – but what I'm talking about is utilizing video to create and deepen relationships.

- **Sharing.** The first step is getting your video up on YouTube. Once it's there, you can share it on social media networks, embed it in your blog, or mail the link wherever you like – and that's powerful. Think of all the product demos you've done at conferences or the number of times you've pitched a product to someone. You can do either of these and more with a YouTube video, and be ready to pass it out like a business card.
- **Viral video.** Viral video doesn't mean watching the video will make you sick, it means that a video has that certain something

that makes people pass it along to their networks, who then pass it along to their networks, and so on – eventually, it spreads the way a virus spreads. It's a good thing; no need to cover your mouth. When people see a viral video, more often than not they wonder "How did this get passed around?" There is some luck involved, but in the end, like anything else, it's about setting yourself up for success and having a strategy. And that starts with you.

HOW YOUR VIDEO CAN GET NOTICED, AND MAYBE "GO VIRAL"

1   The premise

According to YouTube's own fact sheet, "… 24 hours of video viewing is uploaded to YouTube every minute." That's a lot of videos. Yours is not special until you make it special.

2   Content is critical

What makes a video go viral is different from what drives people who watch your video to your site. This section is about the strategy of making something viral, but keep in mind that you need to include the classic call to action to get your viewers to do more than just watch your video. That said, here is how to structure the content of your video to give it the best chance of going viral.

- **Length.** Keep it under 30 seconds. That's one thing that the traditional advertisers figured out for us in the broadcast era.
- **Simple.** Make it simple enough that people can make parodies.
- **Semi-ad.** People don't watch YouTube videos because they are advertisements. So don't make an overt advertisement.
- **Shock value.** People like shock value. Work it in.

- **Sex appeal.** Depending on what your product is, never underestimate what good-looking people do for your video.

3 The "Most Popular" page

You want to be on this page. A significant segment of the tens of millions of YouTube views every day come from people clicking on the Most Popular tab. If your video makes it to this tab, you get traffic. To get on this page, you'll need 50,000+ views. To get this initial critical mass of views, you need to work your network.

- **Blogs.** Do your research and find out who has a blog that is about what your video is about. Send them a personal email asking them to watch and review your video.
- **Forums.** Find the same kind of forums. Get different people in your organization to set up accounts in the forum and start a new thread where you all talk about the new video.
- **Facebook.** Share your video link with as many people as possible. Don't actually upload the video to Facebook, as those views won't count on your YouTube page, but drive traffic to the video on YouTube.
- **Email lists.** You send everything else out to your email lists, send them the video.

4 The title

Use a title that gets people excited, invoking the same kind of words you would use in a classic direct mail campaign. It's more important for the first few days to have a title that is going to draw people in than it is to include your brand or company name. You can change the name of your video at any time.

5   The thumbnail

By default, YouTube uses the exact middle frame of your video as the thumbnail. It's worth your time to make sure that the exact middle of your video is an interesting and compelling picture. You make the call if you want to use something sexy or some other kind of appeal in the frame, but make sure it is an easy to see, intriguing picture.

6   Commenting

Most people watch YouTube videos while they are not logged in, so there are far less comments than there are views. A good way to get the comment thread going is to get people in your office or your friends to log in and comment. Don't be afraid to ask them directly for this. If you are open to it, starting a controversy is a good way to generate interest and draw in other people to comment as well.

8   Tagging

You are more in charge of what other videos come up in the "Related Videos" section than you think. If you choose three unique tags and tag all of your company's videos with those same tags, your videos will come up on the sidebar when a user is watching your video. This is a great strategy to get people to watch more than one of your videos at a time if they are into your video.

EXAMPLES

1   VIRAL VIDEO: NIKE "WRITE THE FUTURE" CAMPAIGN

In 2010, around the time of the World Cup tournament, Nike's "Write the Future" video (www.youtube.com/watch?v=idLG6jh23yE) came out. Even though Nike is not always linked to soccer as their main sport, this video thrust them to the forefront of people's minds during the biggest tournament in competitive soccer. They incorporated players and scenes from a wide variety of teams in the tournament, associating their brand with the entire tournament. With close to 20 million views on YouTube by the end of the World Cup, Nike successfully positioned themselves as exciting and relevant to the growth of soccer popularity worldwide.

2   PERSONALIZATION: MURRAYNEWLANDS.COM

Usually I won't use myself as an example of something I'm writing about, but when I started my blog a few years ago, one of the first things I did was put a video on the homepage. I knew that it would personalize my blog, be a great vehicle for telling people what I was all about, and what I wanted them to do while they were on my page. Here's what I said:

> "Welcome to MurrayNewlands.com. I will be providing you with the very best information about online marketing, how to connect with people, connect with your audience, build your audience, and develop value out of those relationships. And I would really like to connect with you. So please, connect with me through this blog, either by commenting, using the contact form or emailing me, or connecting with me through Facebook or Twitter @MurrayNewlands."

Simple enough. The first sentence lets you know what my blog is about, the second what I want to do, and the third serves as a call to action for what I want my readers to do. It is just 30 seconds long, but it gives people a chance to hear my voice, understand what I am about, and get a sense of what I want them to do on my blog. It's a connection.

3   INTERVIEWS

Interviews used to be the territory of television and radio, but with the proliferation of Flip video cameras and smartphones that can take video, all you need now is someone to hold something in their hand and press record. These videos are easy to make, easy to upload, and are a great way to put a few minutes of a conversation you have with someone at a meeting or a conference on the record. And people love to watch them. This video interview of Chris Brogan (www.youtube.com/watch?v=EquNqi4v_Mk) is a perfect example of a "simple-to-make" video that is just a few minutes in length but connects two people in a public way. Tom O'Rourke, the CEO of O'Rourke Hospitality Marketing, interviews Chris Brogan about website design for hotels. Rather than O'Rourke writing another whitepaper where the content would probably be lost, he conveys the same information through an interview with another social media enthusiast. And you can bet that both parties watched and shared this.

ADVANCED USES

1   USER GENERATED VIDEOS

If you are really a video enthusiast, encouraging your fans or customers to create their own videos either about you, your brand or your products is a great way to get people involved in the social part of video. YouTube has a built-in function that lets people respond to videos, and if you adjust your settings on Facebook, anyone can upload a video to your Facebook Fan Page.

2 REAL TIME

Services like UStream allow anyone to create a live, real-time video feed from any device. If you are speaking at a conference and want to broadcast your speech on your blog, all you need is a partner to stand in the audience with their smartphone, and you have your own live feed right there. For free. If you are at a product launch and you want to give anyone the opportunity to be there over the Internet, you can. Again, for free.

3 CONSUMER REVIEWS

The power of consumer reviews on products or services can be powerful. Think about how most websites cite consumer reviews with a quote and their name (e.g. "I love such-and-such product ..." – C. Jones) but nothing to really prove that this person is, well, a real person. Splicing together a few seconds of endorsement from several satisfied customers on your product or service page will go a long way toward legitimacy and backing up your claims.

 WHAT THE FUTURE HOLDS

Video is only going to get easier to make and easier to share. While there are plenty of Vloggers out there, it's still a niche group that is creating good content on a consistent basis. Here's what I see in the future for businesses.

1   **Your channel.** It's already possible to create a YouTube channel
    where you can publish your own videos and promo materials.
    But what has not started on a wide scale yet is people using video
    the way they use blogs. I expect companies to begin treating
    video as something they can do without dealing with a produc-
    tion team and studio. Why not have Monday morning videos
    with the CEO or Friday wrap-ups? If you have an intern just out
    of college, chances are they have a smartphone that can take the
    video and edit it, then have it uploaded and available within the
    hour.

2   **Crowd-sourced commercials.** People have already taken control
    of their favorite (and least favorite) brands through social media.
    I see more and more people making videos of the products they
    like to use, and I expect that to continue. In a similar way to the
    comments and stories that people post on Facebook Fan Pages, I
    expect videos of products and brands in action to start becoming
    more and more common as smartphones make it easier to make
    those kinds of videos.

3   **Video conversations.** Just as Twitter and Facebook have made
    it possible for brand managers and marketers to have conversa-
    tions with the people that use their products, I expect this to shift
    toward video as smartphones begin to saturate the market. If you
    look at a lot of entertainment marketing, where future trends tend
    to start, this kind of thing is already happening.

TOOLS AND RESOURCES

1 VIDEO TRACKING

Tube Mogul (www.tubemogul.com) and VidMetrix (www.vidmetrix. com) offer great analytics for videos both in and out of YouTube.

2 VIDEO CREATION AND EDITING

iMovie on the Mac is the best and easiest to use format for creating and uploading videos.

3 LIVE STREAMING

UStream (www.ustream.tv) makes a great app for smartphones that allows you to stream content to your personal channel from anywhere.

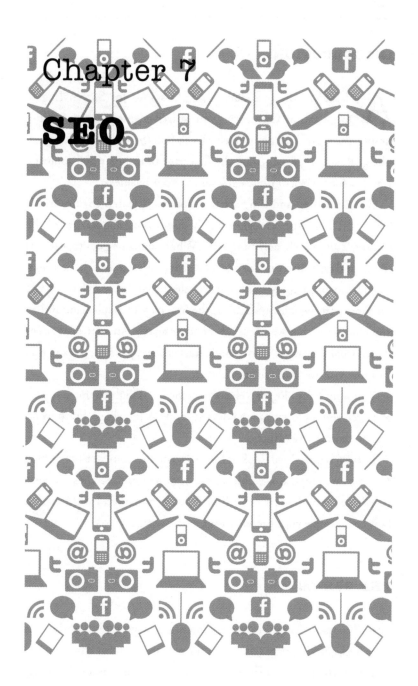

Chapter 7

SEO

INTRODUCTION

As I said in the introduction, SEO stands for Search Engine Optimization. Optimizing your search engine presence is, quite simply, the art of making yourself easy to find through search engines. The goal is to appear high on the first page of results when someone searches for a word or phrase relevant to your business.

Google, Yahoo and Bing are the most used search engines in the UK and USA, with Google roughly comprising about 70% of the market, Yahoo 15%, and Bing 10%. When someone goes to a search engine and types in a word or a set of words ("search terms"), the search engine returns a page of links that are relevant to that search term. For the most part, people only look at the first page of results, and if they don't find what they want, they do another search. And if the page does return what they want, most people start at the top. The top result gets far more visitors than the one below it.

You want your blog or website to come up as high on the first page of search results for as many relevant terms as possible – but how do you do that? There's the rub.

In this chapter I will look at how to structure your website or blog to come up as high as possible on the most relevant searches. Because they have more than two-thirds of the search market, I will focus on how to optimize your presence for Google searches.

THE BASICS

Search engines "scrape" Internet content and aggregate all of the data they find, ranking pages and sites for any search term based on the words on the page and the links from around the web to that page.

In turn, the main SEO tactics are built around "keywords" and "link-building."

KEYWORDS

For your website or blog to be found, you want to appear in the results when someone searches for particular words, and the first thing to do is figure out what keywords are most relevant to your blog or business. If you are starting from scratch, I recommend identifying your keywords before creating your website or blog, as your SEO strategy will be stronger if you are building from a set of keywords.

There are two kinds of keywords – short tail and long tail.

- **Short tail keyword terms** are shorter, more popular terms. For this SEO chapter, examples would be "SEO strategy" or "search engine optimization." These terms are popular searches, probably getting thousands of queries per month.
- **Long tail keyword terms** are made up of multiple words or phrases, like "search engine optimization marketing in the UK," or "search engine keyword strategies 2011." Long tail keywords tend to have lower monthly search volumes, maybe in the hundreds of queries or less, but are much easier to get on the first page of search results.

I recommend starting your SEO process by selecting five keywords to work with. It will allow you to stay focused on making the strategy work for a small sample, and then taking what you learn and applying it to more keywords as you grow your SEO strategy.

Using this chapter as an example, I may select "SEO, search engine optimization, search engine keywords, search engine ranking, and Google SEO." What you select for your business or blog is entirely based on what you focus on and what you want people to find you for. For example, if your blog is about horse racing, you would want to select terms like "horse racing, horse races, horse racing blog, horse race, and horse racing articles."

Once you have selected some keywords to start with, it's time to start building.

THINGS TO CONSIDER

1   Domain name

Google favors domain names, meaning they give your domain name a lot of weight. If my blog were called searchengineoptimization.com, I have a big advantage over someone else writing about SEO whose blog is called strategytime.com. Many of the best URLs are already taken, so you need to be creative in choosing your domain. While search-engineoptimization.com is no longer available, seobymurray.com may be, or seostrategies.com. Having a main keyword in your domain name will be a big help when Google looks at your page.

Additionally, when people are searching for a website, there is a brand trust in the mind of the user when the URL contains the name. If I find a blog called seostrategies.com, I will know that that is what the blog is about, as opposed to strategytime.com, which tells me nothing about what kind of strategy or topic the blog is going to be about – how would I know if it's SEO or horse racing strategy?

If you are creating the website for your company, your best bet is to choose a domain name that is your company name, and if that is taken, choose something that contains your company name.

2   Content

Quite simply, you need to have what people are looking for in order for them to spend time on your site. Before you launch a new website or blog, start creating the content so that you have a stock to publish. Creating a content plan and schedule is also an important step when you are starting out, as search engines like it when a page or blog is frequently updated with fresh content.

3   Content structure

Structuring your pages with titles and search terms in the URLs and titles will increase your search engine ranking. If you are creating a website, naming the page with a keyword (i.e. seobymurray.com/searchengineoptimization) will help that page rank for that term. If you are writing posts, setting your blog up so that the title of your post will become part of the URL (i.e. seobymurray.com/how-to-do-seo) will help that individual post rank well for that term.

4   Content link value

Your content has to provide value. Anyone can pump out lots of web pages or post blog articles every day. While creating pages and posts that have value to the people that read them is tougher, it will keep people on your site longer, encourage them to link to your content, and raise the overall influence and brand presence of your site or blog. Provocative, informative, topical, and contentious pages or blog posts have all proven to be things that people want to link to.

5   Internal linking

Search engines like links because they show that a page is offering something of value. Linking within your own website to specific pages will help those pages appear higher in search results. Likewise, linking later blog entries back to earlier posts that are central to your message and topic will help those earlier entries appear higher on the results.

6   External linking

This is something to think about from the beginning, even though it comes later in the process. When other people link to your web pages or blog posts from their sites, it shows search engines that your pages or posts have value. Making other people aware of your content, and even actively asking for links to your pages, will help get those inbound links. Publishing it through social media and giving people the opportunity to link to it will help expand your presence.

 HOW TO USE IT IN PRACTICE

Now that you know the basics of why SEO is important, let's look at how to make it happen.

1   DOMAIN NAMES

When you go to register your domain name, ideally you buy something that is relevant to your own business, topic and country. I recommend starting your search with a domain sale service like GoDaddy.com. But do you buy your own name, or do you buy your company? Your name is personal, and business done through social media is increasingly personal. If you own your own business, buying your name can be a good option, though there is no resale opportunity. If you are looking for your company or for a new service, you want to buy a domain with the company or service name in it.

If the name you want is taken and you can't buy it straight away, check a website like Sedo.com that people use to resell and trade domain URLs to see if yours is available. Keep in mind that the older the domain name, the more weight and value the search engines will give to it. "Way Back When" (waybackwhen.com) is a good resource for seeing domain name history, from how long they have been around to what content they hosted in the past.

If you are buying an old domain name, don't delete the old pages, rather redirect them to your new domain, otherwise you lose the value of the pages, which is also valuable because of all the internal and external links. You can register a domain name for one year or many years, some search engines favor domain names registered for many years.

2 CONTENT

Once you've got your domain name, it's time to start creating content. When writing content with SEO in mind, what you create still needs to be valuable to the reader. Writing content just for SEO purposes will get you some traffic in the short-term, but it won't endear you to your readers, and they won't spend much time with your post, refer you, or link to your site.

That said, "on-page" SEO is valuable, and when you have a page that you want to rank well, here is how you start:

1   **Keyword research.** Your first step is researching and choosing the right keywords for your goals. The Google keyword tool is a great resource for finding the right short and long tail keywords to use in content. Review your competitors' websites and see what terms they are optimizing on their websites. I recommend choosing terms that have less competition when you are starting out.

When you are considering what to title an individual page, research how many searches for those terms happen on Google every month. You want to choose a keyword that gets some traffic, but not so much that you have no chance of making the first page of search engine results.

2 **Title.** Make the name of the page URL and the page title the term that you want to optimize for. It's best to keep the title short, and to put the term that you are optimizing for at the beginning. For example, if you are optimizing for "SEO Strategy," make the name of your page "SEO Strategy Tips" rather than "10 Tips for a Good SEO Strategy." Then, make sure the term that you want to optimize the content for is in the first paragraph.

3 **Formatting.** When you are writing a page, it's good to use headings and section titles in the page. Wherever it makes sense, use your keyword(s) as section titles, **embolden** them, and make them an H1–H6 header. If you are linking out from your page to another one, make sure you hyperlink only the text that contains the keyword(s) you want to be ranked. For example, if I write a page about what I'm working on and say, "I work with clients on SEO strategy," I'll hyperlink the words "SEO strategy" to my SEO strategy page, rather than just "SEO," "strategy," or the entire sentence.

4 **Sharing.** Once content is published, share it on social media and bookmarking sites. It is more likely that Google will find the article fast and they will carry some SEO weight, even if only a small amount.

5 **Additional tips.**
- Make a video with the name of the article and page it in YouTube. Place the video in the article and link back to the article from YouTube.

- Make the article at least 250 words. Google likes articles that are at least that long.
- Repeating the keyword will help, but keep it to no more than 30 other words to one keyword. And make sure to offer value in the article, not just keyword repetition.
- Look in your own log to see what people are finding your site through. If relevant, create more content around those search terms. You'd find this in your own weblogs and/or Google analytics.

3   CONTENT STRUCTURE

You want to structure content in such a way that it can be found easily by humans and ranked highly by search engines. The main things that you want people to find you for should be linked from and to your home page. Just as in the structure of a library, humans and search engines want content that is similar to be clustered together so that it is easy to understand.

4   LINK VALUE

Create content that is valuable and that people will want to link to. This can be things like top ten lists, whitepapers, or presentations. The best way to start thinking about it is asking yourself what you would want to find in your business area, and then create a web page about that. People love to see comparisons of different services, How-to's on difficult topics, or anything that makes their job easier. This is a great way to getting external links to your site, and the first step in becoming a thought leader.

5   INTERNAL LINKING

Linking different pages on your own site to each other, or from a new blog entry to an old blog entry, is a great way to get your content noticed by the search engines. If you have a blog, chances are you will be writing about a similar topic area over time, and there will be opportunities for you to reference yourself. When you do this (and you should as much as possible), make the hyperlinked text one of your keywords. For example, if you are optimizing for "SEO Strategy," link that term in your new blog entry to an old post about some aspect of SEO strategy. This link will benefit your old post.

Another part of this tactic is to have 5–10 core posts or website pages that you want to focus on optimizing for. This way you can do all of the on-page SEO really well, repeatedly link to it from your subsequent blog posts, and focus on getting external links to that page or post as well …

6   EXTERNAL LINKING

Google loves external links. It means that whatever content you have created is valuable enough to other people that they want to link to it. So how do you get external links from other blogs and websites?

1 **Value.** I've talked about it a lot in this section, but nothing beats creating a post that is valuable to the people who read it.
2 **Social media.** If people don't know about your post, they won't read it and can't link to it. Posting it to social media networks is a great way to publicize your new post or a specific web page, and that raises the chance that someone will find it and want to link to it.

3   **Give and you shall receive.** Link to other blogs from your posts
    and they are more likely to do the same back to yours.

4   **Link exchange.** Know what terms you want to rank for and ask
    people to link to you from those words. Many bloggers who are
    trying to build up their own sites will do a link exchange, where
    they will link to you on a specific term if you link back to them on
    a term they are trying to build SEO for.

5   **Guest posting.** Writing a guest post on another blog is great
    for many reasons, from becoming a thought leader to building
    business relationships. For SEO it helps because you are typically
    invited to write a short bio at the end of the article and you can link
    back to yourself from a term of your choosing.

EXAMPLES

CHRIS BROGAN (WWW.CHRISBROGAN.COM)

This is a good example of a blog that gets a lot of external linking. He
gets it because he publishes regularly and his content provides a lot of
value. He also does a lot of speaking at various conferences and meetups about what he does, which is putting the human back in business
communications. He also makes a habit of helping people with their
blogs and is incredibly active on social media. All of that means that
people know his name, and his name is his domain. Do a Google search
for the word "Chris" and see where he comes up (this only works if you
are in the USA …).

HORSE RACING

Going back to my earlier example of horse racing, here is a set of results from a Google search for "horse racing."

1   www.espn.go.com/horse-racing/ – ESPN is an international sports information source, and chances are their horse racing page has an enormous number of external links.
2   www.en.wikipedia.org/wiki/Horse_racing – Wikipedia has much the same story, in that there are an incredible number of external links referring to their pages on every topic.
3   www.horseracing.com/ – True to form, the third ranking page has the words "horse racing" in the domain.

ADVANCED USES

ANALYTICS AND MONITORING

Keeping track of where your pages and posts appear on search engine results will let you know if your SEO efforts are working, but they can be time consuming. It is worth looking into professional monitoring services to see if the cost of paying someone else to monitor both your search engine results and your reputation are worth using that time to build your business in other ways.

SOCIAL MEDIA

When people talk about advanced SEO, many times it will seem like they are talking about online PR, and in a way they are. Because social media is becoming not just a place where people connect with each other and find news but also a place where they actively go to find recommendations, social media offers an entirely different way to think about the concept of "search." Yes, ranking high in search engine results is still essential, but it's also important to be active on and have a good reputation on social media networks. People go to places like Twitter and Facebook to ask their friends for recommendations, so it is to your advantage to have a presence on those networks, not just to connect with potential and current customers, but to be easy to link to and refer when people are "searching" for a service or product through their social networks. Think of it as networking and public relations where people already are, so when they need to make a recommendation to a friend, you are at the top of their mind. There is increasing evidence that some search engines favor content which has been shared in social media sites by users.

MULTIMEDIA CONTENT CREATION

Sites like YouTube, Flickr and Twitter have their own internal search functions, and coming up high in the search results on these sites is becoming as important as coming up high on Google, Yahoo or Bing. Using consistent keywords across all of the media that you create, and making sure that you create fresh content in each of them is a great way to make sure that no matter where people are looking for a business or blog like yours, you are part of the results.

GUEST BLOGGING

We already talked about how important external links are, and one great way to get those external links is to actively pursue guest blogging opportunities. If you can find bloggers who write about your industry, chances are they are looking for people to write about it and post on their blog. It gives them a day off from writing content, and it helps vary the voice on their blog. Most search engines only permit each site to have one position for each key term. Having content on a number of websites written by you, which can then rank in different positions means that you have more chance of reaching the attention of your audience. Other sites may rank higher than yours in search engines and therefore have more chance of being seen by searchers.

 WHAT THE FUTURE HOLDS

As more and more people are creating websites and blogs, there is more and more content on the web. This makes search engine optimization an ongoing challenge. At the same time, there are more and more strategies and opportunities through social media and the localization of web content.

Here are a few ways that SEO is evolving:

1   **Social media SEO.** Services like Facebook and Twitter continue to expand, and search engines are beginning to display social media content as part of their results. Using keywords in your social media posts will be recognized by Google, and they will appear in the search results. This means that your SEO strategy is a living process, and coordinating your site SEO with your social media posting is beneficial in search results.

2   **Real-time SEO.** Many people are starting to use Twitter as a search engine in and of itself. For more on this, read the Twitter section in the social media chapter of this book. Using relevant #hashtags in Twitter is a great way to keep your content at the top

of Twitter's real-time search. Also, content curation services like Evri (www.evri.com) are scraping a variety of news and social media sources for the most recent, relevant content on the web, and this kind of automated content curation is only going to become more important as the web gets more crowded.

3   **Local SEO.** As more people get on the web, it is becoming important to rank high in search results when people look for business or content that is relevant to them locally. Optimizing your website and blog to be found locally begins with using your city or country name in long tail keywords, as well as incorporating search terms that are specific to the local groups and interests near where you live and work.

TOOLS AND RESOURCES

There are many services, some of which I have mentioned in this chapter, that will help you create and maintain quality SEO.

1   **Sedo.** Sedo is a domain broker that will help you purchase a URL if it is owned but not being used (www.sedo.com).

2   **Way Back When.** This website will show you the age of a URL and what it has been used for in the past (www.archive.org).

3   **Alexa.** Alexa is a web information portal that will show you the rankings of every website and blog. It is very helpful to monitor your traffic and keep track of your progress (www.alexa.com).

4   **Google keyword tool.** This tool allows you to see how many searches a given keyword gets per month, which is helpful in selecting your keywords (www.adwords.google.com/select/KeywordToolExternal).

5   **Google trends.** This free site lets you see the top recent search terms, which can be helpful when you are writing blog entries (www.google.com/trends).

6   **Blog.** (www.stateofsearch.com).

7   **SEO tool.** (www.majesticseo.com).

Chapter 8

Email
Marketing

INTRODUCTION

Email marketing has been slowly taking over from direct mail marketing for over a decade, and there is no shortage of innovation in the field. It's about a lot more than just redesigning print mailers online – it is about developing new relationships with customers and maintaining those that already exist.

One of the most important social media marketing mantras is that you need to talk to people where they already are, and that applies to email marketing very well. Email is well established: almost everyone with a computer and Internet access has an email address, and the first thing most people do when they log onto a computer is check their email. That makes email a powerful tool in any kind of online marketing initiative. Statistics vary as to the actual numbers, but it's established that three out of four email marketers have integrated social email into their campaigns.

I think Chris Brogan put the value of email in perspective when he said:

> "Only 5% of people have a relationship with a brand through social media, whereas 95% of people have a relationship with a brand through email marketing."

Beyond the basics, the transition from direct postal mail to email is really the evolution of this medium through integration and synchronization with social media campaigns. Connecting people with further content and sharing options can drastically increase reach and grow email lists.

But it's more than that. Brian Solis is right when he says that "Email is technically the largest, untapped, social network in the world." The connections are there – your job as an email marketer is to figure out how to make people use them.

THE BASICS

Think of your email marketing campaign as a value exchange. If you want someone's business, you need to offer a good reason. But how do you drawn on the largest untapped social media network in the world? The first question to ask yourself is, "Why should people receive and open your email?" Why should people want it? Spend a good amount of your design time with this question. Then, know that it needs to stand out.

Email marketing has great potential; if you get your message right it can spread around the Internet. According to StrongMail's *Influence Benchmark Report* from 2009, email accounts for 86% of all sharing activity within direct marketing programs – making it the preferred sharing method over such popular methods as Facebook (6%) and Twitter (4%). What does this mean for you? It means that when people find information they want to share, they share it through email. It means you need to send things that people want to share. It means that you include a call to action to ask people to share the content from an email on their social networks, be that Twitter or Facebook, or other networks, from MySpace and Bebo to smaller niche online communities.

Your first task is to build a relationship of trust through email. People decide how and where they want to connect. Email can be a dialogue between your company and your customers and potential customers. It is a personal way to engage in long-term customer relationship management (CRM), stay relevant and cultivate brand affinity. With the growing convergence of social media and email, combining the two allows you to offer choice and not only speak to people where they are (email), but empower them to share on their chosen network.

WHAT TO THINK ABOUT TO MAKE YOUR EMAIL MARKETING CAMPAIGN WORK

Email is a great way to reach people because it is so popular, yes, but that also means that you have plenty of competition for attention. You'll need to be targeted, relevant, and to the point. There is so much information out there, and people rely on recommendations. Once you start your campaign, your job is to figure out who shares information, when and why, and how you can cultivate a relationship with those people.

- **Expectations.** Make sure you are meeting and exceeding recipient expectations – this should be in the design as well as the content. People get dozens of emails every day and only read a small percentage of them. If people come to expect poor content from you they will become blind to your emails and delete them without reading them or mark them as spam. The only way to deal with this is to make sure that you have great content.
- **Lists.** Ideally, you build your own double-opt-in list (see below). Your customer's emails are the best email addresses. Some people find free giveaways are a great way of collecting email addresses, although you can wind up building it with people who are only looking for a handout (I shall say more about this later). That way it's yours and you don't need to pay anyone to use or own it. You can buy or rent lists, which will get you a lot of names and addresses, but you need to be careful not to be perceived as "spammy" when those

people receive your emails. If expanding to those people grows your business, that's a good thing – if it just gets your message out to more inboxes, you need to be careful.

- **Opt-in and out.** A double-opt-in list is when people first sign up to the email list of their own volition, whether in person at an event or through something online. That is opting-in. Then, the first email they receive is telling them that they have been added to that email list, and that if they click a link, they are agreeing to be on the email list. That is opt-in number two.

  It's not just important because you will have people on your list who you want to be on your list – it's important because companies are developing sophisticated software that identifies spam email, and because email list software often makes it a preference, or even a requirement, that the lists you host on their service are double-opt-in because they don't want to be held responsible for spam.

  At the same time, it is important to make it easy to opt-out or unsubscribe so that people who want to stop receiving your emails can do so easily. The number one complaint that people have about email campaigns is that it is difficult to get out when they want to get out. Not making it easy to unsubscribe is a sure way to get complaints and a bad name for your campaign.

- **List hygiene.** It sounds funny, sure, but it is critical to keep your list clean and well manicured. You want to get rid of duplicates, addresses that don't work anymore, and make sure that it is kept orderly and up to date.

- **Content relevancy.** With so much email flying around, it's critical that your content is relevant to the people who receive it. This ties your lists to your content in a very real way. Think about how you treat your own inbox – how much time do you spend with an email that doesn't grab you? Or one that isn't tailored to your needs?

- **Tracking.** It's important to know who has opened and who has clicked on your emails. Monitor and track what is being sent out vs what people are clicking on and passing on – this is how you will know what is working and what isn't. It's how you figure out who your influencers are, and it's how you'll know who to target for your next campaign, and what worked and what didn't so that you can be even more effective the next time around.

Email marketing still is going to have an impact for many years to come, even though the younger generation seem to have more use for social media. The key take-away on the shift from direct post to email to social media is that there isn't really a disconnect, there is a convergence. While some people are predicting the death of email, it is likely to be important for some time. Statistically, most people are still more connected to brands and each other rather than anything else. People are seeing increasing response and sharing rates for emails that have social media sharing options, or social media subscribe options. Keep in mind that people also share the bad stuff, so it's important to remember that nothing is more important than creating and sending out good content.

 HOW TO USE IT IN PRACTICE

When you are setting up your email campaign, you look at three things: planning, execution and tracking.

PLANNING

1   **Audience and purpose.** With any marketing campaign, you want to establish who you are trying to reach and what you want

them to do. One thing that hasn't changed in the transition from direct postal to email marketing campaigns is that you want to connect with the right people and have a clear call to action that they understand and can do easily. You should spend more time figuring out who to contact, how to contact them and what to say than you do with how the email looks.

2   **Research.** Know what your competitors are doing. Get an idea for how they are approaching similar products so that you can take what you like and implement it, and also know what you can do differently to make your campaign stand out. This means everything from subscribing to competitors' email lists to researching blog posts by them where they may write about their successes.

Ongoing broad research into the evolving techniques of social media within email marketing is invaluable. The field is literally evolving and changing every day, so keeping up on your reading to stay abreast of what's new in the industry will give you new ideas and enable you to take advantage of any new techniques. You don't want to stay in your cubicle cave from planning through execution.

3   **Content.** Once you have your audience and purpose established, it's time to start writing and designing. Whether you have a staff writer or are doing the writing yourself, make sure to give yourself enough time to write, edit, and rewrite the copy several times before it needs to go into your email. Closely consider content relevancy, making sure that what you write is tailored to the people who will be reading it.

Because you should be creating an email marketing campaign that is as social as you can make it, make sure all of the content is social media friendly. Whether this means including social media sharing buttons or specific messaging that you want people to include in their posts, the key is to make it clear and concise.

Formatting is also critical. Ideally you want to send the email both as text and as html, so that different people's browsers can all open the emails, regardless of what they are doing. Also, make sure your email will work on mobile devices. Many platforms provide the user with the ability to create text and HTML versions of the email. These are both sent at the same time and the program that receives the email and displays it to the user will only display the version (text or HTML) which the user has set as their preference. Most email tools have the facility for you to send these messages separately to your own account and view them separately. Many people also send test emails to themselves and friends to test compatibility.

Finally, test your campaign. Do audio and visual testing before you start sending a campaign out – you have to know what it's going to look like in everyone's browser, and fixing issues before someone sends you an email about it is the best way to do that.

EXECUTION

1   **Choosing an email marketing provider.** If you are doing an email marketing campaign of any substantial size, I highly recommend that you find a hosting service. Unless email marketing is all you are doing, the logistics behind a large-scale campaign take a lot of time and expertise and can be overwhelming. I have my recommendations for providers listed in the Tools and Resources section.

2   **Timing.** It seems simple, but it is critically important. You want your call-to-action to be timed well so that people receive and can act on it immediately. Think about what day of the week you

want your emails going out, what time of day you want people to receive them, and allow them the time to respond. Be conscious of holidays, time zones and the timing of campaigns that your competitors are running.

3 **Customer service.** When you run an email marketing campaign, you are trying to increase either your traffic or sales to a particular site or project. When it works, you'll get the sales and the traffic, but you'll also get a rise in the number of people who are confused or are having issues with wherever you are sending them. Make sure that you increase the number of people and time spent responding to and dealing with customer service issues appropriately.

TRACKING

At the end of the day, you want to know that your email marketing campaign is working – and for most people that means, "Am I making sales?" Email marketing campaigns continue to return the best numbers against any other type of direct marketing. According to the StrongMail report, sharing offers via email generated a 36.8% conversion rate, making it the highest performing sharing channel – nearly doubling what blogs and badges returned, at 20.5%. While success and key numbers for your campaign will vary slightly depending on your goals, there are several key numbers that you want to track.

1 **Email open-rate.** Just because you send out 100,000 emails doesn't mean 100,000 people are going to open them. The first key number to note is how many people actually open the emails that you send out. If this is your first email marketing campaign or you are working with new lists, you'll find this to be a solid benchmark number on which to gauge your success and future

growth. Most email marketing platforms will tell you the number of people who have opened the email. Note that none of these are 100% accurate.

2 **Conversions.** How many people do what your email call to action asks them to do is the ultimate statistic that will tell you if your campaign is a success. Monitoring this will be down to the achievement of the goals that you set for your campaign; for example, how many people called the number you asked them to in the email. In the email marketing field, we call that a conversion. Being clear about that call to action and making it something that you can easily monitor, track and report is critical to understanding if your campaign has been successful.

3 **Social media sharing.** Understanding how many people share your email content through the social media sharing options (you should be integrating these!) will give you benchmarks of another level of reaction to your program content. People share content with their social media networks in order to make recommendations to their friends – high numbers in this category can be more meaningful than individual responses in the long run.

4 **Online monitoring.** There are a number of services that will monitor keywords across all content areas on the Internet. In addition to tracking the response rates to your emails, it is useful to track the online chatter about your company and product across social networks, blogs, and any other place people may be talking about you online. It will allow you to pinpoint where your campaign is sparking good conversations that you want to be a part of, as well as conversations that may not paint what you are doing in the best light. Either way, monitoring the Internet as a whole will allow you to get involved in those conversations.

5 **Personal feedback.** It's not all about the numbers. Understanding that your email campaigns are talking to real people and that they will be contacting you is critical. Make sure that you are responding to the people who take the time to email you with questions or any other kind of feedback – good or bad. The folks who take the time to do that are probably the same "influencers" you are looking to connect with on your campaign, and in many ways how they feel about what you're doing will determine your success.

For all of these numbers, your best bet is to integrate your email campaign with a provider who has a robust tracking system already in place so that you have the numbers at your fingertips.

EXAMPLES

1 EMAIL MARKETING SERVICE

A service like StrongMail's Influencer solution will let you do everything I've been talking about. Have a look at this solution or one like it to make your next email marketing campaign more effective.

StrongMail Influencer enables you to integrate social media into email campaigns to make them viral marketing campaigns. The idea is to encourage people to share via their preferred social media channel – again, first talking to people where they already are (on email) and then calling them to act on the social media networks where they spend their time (Facebook, Twitter, etc.).

While you can try doing this on your own, the advantage of doing this with a provider like StrongMail is that they will have automatic and robust reporting. Regardless of whether you use StrongMail or another provider, the ability to identify your key influencers and target them with the right kind of messaging makes email marketing not only more relevant, but more successful. In kind, it gives more power to the eventual social media sharing that you are asking for.

2   EMAIL MARKETING CAMPAIGNS

Kraft Foods: www.wdfm.com/marketing-viewpoints/future-email.php

Kraft Foods is a great example of a large company reaching out to their active customer base for feedback and then acting on that feedback. Within their email programs, they periodically include surveys and then share the results with their subscribers. One example I saw was that they asked their email subscribers if they would be interested in receiving mobile updates when they are in a store to help with shopping – 95% said no. That enabled Kraft to save a lot of time and energy by not creating a service that their active customers didn't actually want. They also worked within the social media mantra of being transparent by sharing those results with their email subscriber base.

CSN Stores

One of the best uses of an active email subscriber base is to get subscribers to use their influence and friend network to create new customers. CSN Stores, a competitor of huge sites like Amazon and eBay, ran a successful referral program as part of a 2009 email marketing campaign.

They asked their most active customers to refer friends through social media links. Members who referred a friend received a $15 credit in their CSN Rewards account when a friend enrolled and made a purchase. It was a huge success. It's a classic tactic adapted to the social media sharing abilities of cutting-edge email marketing campaigns.

I think each of these examples shows a powerful way of making email marketing social: asking customers for their opinions to customize future content and incentivizing social media sharing: personalization and a reason to share.

ADVANCED USES

- **Integration.** Launching an email marketing campaign that is integrated with your other social media outlets and your web presence is a tall order, as it takes a lot of time, planning and monitoring to make it happen. But if you are looking for a way to make your campaign as effective as possible, it's a great option. Doing a lot of things all at once *will* have more influence than doing the same amount of things over a one or two month period. Why? Because you will be everywhere.

- **Inbound marketing.** Integrating your campaign also opens the door for your outbound email campaign to grow into an inbound marketing campaign. Do it right and people will start to recognize your name and those social media shares will lead to people finding you, learning more about your products, and find out what you are up to. At that point, you want to have things ready for them to find and get interested in. Inbound marketing works when people seek you out and *find* something of value to them. It's your job to have those things available on your website and social networks, whether they are additional products, whitepapers or active communities.

"When it comes to integrating email and social media, there are two things to consider. First is the technical aspect of adding Like, Tweet, and other social share buttons to your outgoing emails. Many service providers, including Constant Contact, make this easy to do in a couple clicks. By including share buttons in your emails, recipients can endorse your message with the click of a button and share it with their own friends and followers.

By making it easy for customers to share your emails with their social media circle, you can extend the reach of your marketing content far beyond your original distribution list."

Eric Groves, Constant Contact

Eric says that by leveraging your existing email marketing content to feed your social media channels, you can speed up the customer acquisition process since your messages will reach more people more quickly. "Who knows who your next best customer is better than your current customers?" Eric explains. Making it easy for your customers to tell their friends, family, and colleagues – via social sharing of your existing content – is an easy way to immediate word-of-mouth marketing.

In order to get people to share your messages you have to give them content that's relevant and engaging, as this chapter has discussed. Part of creating engaging content though is to start conversations. Engaging email content gets readers to think and want to react. No matter what your line of business or what you're discussing, start the conversation in your email and direct readers to your Facebook page, Twitter, or other social channel to continue the conversation. By beginning the conversation in email and continuing it in social media, your customers will help you build an active social media presence, which prospects will see and want to become a part of.

Eric also reminds social media marketers to make sure they're driving new social media fans and followers back to your email list by occasionally posting links to their email signup forms or adding a "join my mailing list" application to their Facebook page. This helps complete the customer acquisition cycle.

 WHAT THE FUTURE HOLDS

- **Social media.** I've already talked about many of the options for turning an email into content that people can share with their networks, and for this kind of integration to continue. The evolution of social media capabilities within email will allow the emails you send out to be seamlessly shared across social media networks. With the rise of location-based marketing and messaging, I expect that kind of behavior-based information to influence who gets what kind of emails, or for location-based services to establish newsletters that are tailored to the places users frequent.

- **Focus on subscribers.** It seems intuitive that you would tailor what you send out to the people who want it, but traditional email marketing campaigns tend to focus on numbers rather than recipients, viewing subscriber numbers as a growing pool of people to mine for conversions and sales. The paradigm shift within email marketing is to look at who has opted-in or subscribed to your email list and what kind of information they want. The focus needs to be on what your subscribers are interested in hearing, not what you want to tell them. Look for a rise in actively asking for feedback within email marketing campaigns and diversifying the prongs of a campaign. Businesses are customizing their email marketing to local and national audiences, and that kind of customization serves to make the content more relevant, which in turn makes recipients even more likely to share – it's an evolving win–win for everyone involved.

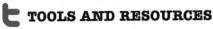 **TOOLS AND RESOURCES**

RECOMMENDED EMAIL MARKETING PROVIDERS

- AWebber (www.awebber.com). Great for small businesses.
- Constant Contact (www.constantcontact.com). Great for small and medium businesses.
- StrongMail (www.strongmail.com). Great for larger and enterprise scale businesses.

Chapter 9

Affiliate Marketing

INTRODUCTION

What is affiliate marketing? I can't count the number of times someone has asked me that. I've been in affiliate marketing for a long time and the details of that answer has changed almost as many times as it's been asked, but the basics have remained the same. Simply put, affiliate marketing is a network of independent vendors or people marketing the same product or service in return for a commission on sales. An affiliate is often a website owner who earns a commission for referring sales leads or conversions through that website to a merchant or business.

Not too long ago it was a niche, specialist art form, and as the Internet has grown, so has affiliate marketing – it's now a much more mainstream approach encompassing business-to-business products and services as well as consumer needs.

An affiliate business is just like a business of any other type. There are lots of one-man band affiliates in affiliate marketing, and it is true that you can start an affiliate business with very little overhead from your bedroom, but they can grow very fast from there. There are plenty of large operations that started as one-man band affiliate companies. There are also large companies that become affiliate marketers for other companies or products because a significant portion of their traffic is interested in this area. Affiliate marketing is a great way to earn extra money while connecting people to the products they need and want already.

With the advances in the security and ease of online purchasing, the growing amount of choice and quality in online stores, and the normalization of shopping and buying things online, affiliate marketing is something that many businesses are starting to utilize. Preparing a company for affiliate marketing, selecting an affiliate network and recruiting affiliates can seem like a daunting task to those unfamiliar with the territory; however the rewards can be significant.

In this chapter I will discuss how to choose an affiliate network, recruit affiliates, create offers and manage a program. It's a lot to learn, but it's not so different from managing any kind of sales force. It's about real people selling good products with a particular set of tools. And the great thing about the affiliate marketing community is that it's full of great people who, like you, once had to learn everything from scratch – and they're more than willing to help you out.

THE BASICS

An affiliate is someone who uses their web presence to drive sales traffic to another business. The affiliate earns money for each sale (conversion) that they bring to the company. For example: Company A (a merchant/advertiser) pays a commission to Company B (an affiliate) for generating sales, leads, or clicks from a graphic or text link located on Company B's (affiliate) website or Internet reach, which could include email, or social media presence.

Affiliate marketing benefits merchants by producing results-based sales or leads. Growing your business with minimal risk through results-based customer acquisition is attractive to many companies because they only pay for what they get. If affiliates do not make sales or generate leads or if they have a bad day, they don't get paid.

There are a variety of different ways for affiliate marketing to work.

TYPES OF AFFILIATES

Content affiliates

Content affiliates have traditionally worked with banners and text links on their websites to drive traffic to affiliate merchants' websites.

Content affiliates are now increasingly collecting email lists and many will have newsletters which they can use to drive traffic to your affiliate marketing programs.

A content affiliate could be a one-man band with a blog about a very niche subject such as their band. Some of these affiliates can be very small revenue generators. There are however content affiliate bloggers who drive thousands of pounds or dollars of sales per month. There are also an increasingly large number of very big content affiliates who were traditional publishers selling advertising and now also use affiliate links to monetize their content.

Content affiliates may also be able to take a feed of products from your website and integrate those products into their website. You can then provide them with dynamic content updates to make sure that they are featuring your latest products. Content affiliates benefit from the updated content you provide for their websites.

However it is done, affiliate marketing is on the cutting edge of what it means to do business on the Internet.

Reward affiliates

Reward sites are communities where affiliates share the affiliate commission with users. It works because it makes the situation even more of a win–win for everyone involved.

Reward affiliate sites benefit from consumer interaction and consumers' desire for money off. Some merchants choose not to work with rewards affiliates because they see it as reducing their brand value, not to mention their cut of the commissions.

Think of it as Air Miles where you can earn miles when you purchase anything online that has an affiliate program. Reward affiliate sites can be great for selling retail products online. There are some very large reward affiliates in the UK and US. In the UK, reward affiliates tend to be called "cashback affiliates" and their websites are called cashback sites. In the US they are called "reward affiliates" or "incentive affiliates."

Note while reward sites can be a good source of traffic, some reward sites can suffer from sending fraudulent traffic as individual users try and gain the system to make commissions without really making purchases.

Pay per click (PPC)

A pay-per-click (PPC) affiliate is a person or a company that drives traffic to affiliate offers. PPC affiliates buy ads on Google, Facebook, Myspace and other websites and use that to drive sales.

If a PPC affiliate pays less in clicks than the commission they make from the sale of the item they make a profit; if not, they take a loss. There are affiliates who have made millions of pounds or dollars doing this.

For example: if your company sells blue roses, the affiliate would buy clicks on the paid right-hand column on Google for the term "buy blue roses." The user would then be directed via a landing page to your site to buy blue roses. If it costs 10p or 10c per click and one in ten converts, it costs them £1 or $1 to make one sale. If they are paid £2 or $2 per sale then they would make a profit of £1 or $1 per sale.

HOW TO USE IT IN PRACTICE

Affiliate marketing benefits merchants by engaging hundreds and possibly thousands of online marketing experts who contribute their time, money, skills and resources to grow a merchant's business on a performance-only basis. There are not many spheres where you can truly engage leading experts from all around the world to promote your business at their own risk.

Affiliate marketing benefits merchants by creating large-scale brand awareness for a merchant's products and services online. This brand awareness is not paid for directly by the merchant, who only pays when a sale is made or a lead delivered. Many merchants see this as risk-free advertising. The brand awareness created through affiliate marketing is arguably as effective in the growth of some companies as the sales made directly by the affiliates.

Affiliate marketing benefits the merchant through promotions innovation for a product or service. Affiliates are experts at staying on the cutting-edge of online marketing and finding innovative ways to promote merchants online.

IN HOUSE AFFILIATE SOFTWARE OR USING AN AFFILIATE NETWORK

If you are going to track and pay affiliates for making sales you need some software and a payment system. There are solutions you can use yourself such as www.hasoffers.com, many people chose to use an affiliate network. Affiliate networks run the affiliate tracking and payment systems for many different companies and have the advantage of having relationships in place with thousands of affiliates. Many people new to affiliate marketing choose to use a network because it enables them to concentrate on the marketing of their products and removes the technical burden. Affiliate networks can also provide great promotional exposure for your company among their existing affiliate base. When choosing an affiliate network I would recommend looking on the affiliate forums and seeing what others say about them. In the UK, Affiliate Window (www.affiliatewindow.com) has market dominance.

Recruiting affiliates

Approaching new affiliates is just like approaching any other kind of partner – you begin by learning as much as you can about him or her. Because online affiliate marketing happens online, this can be easier than doing a background check on a potential employee or other business partner. There are some affiliates who are very informal and like to be approached in an informal way. There are other affiliates who are very formal and would much prefer a standard business-like approach. Affiliate forums and networking events are great ways to find affiliates and find out more about what they want.

EXAMPLES

AMAZON.COM

This is one of the oldest, most visible, and still one of the best examples of a successful, scalable affiliate marketing program (www.affiliate-program.amazon.com). When a book club website reviews a book and recommends next week's reading, if they refer a book club member to Amazon for a purchase, the book club gets a commission.

REWARD AFFILIATES

There are a number of rewards and points sites you can look at to get a feel for how they work. If you are a member of www.mypoints.com every time you buy online you get points, and you can use these points to get other products or discounts. See also www.sunshinerewards.com.

ADVANCED USES

SOCIAL MEDIA AFFILIATES

It's becoming ubiquitous, so you may wonder why I think of it as an "advanced" use. I would say for exactly that reason. Social media is about real people interacting with real people.

Social media is the ideal way for connecting real people with good deals on the products they want. If you, as a person with a social media profile, can establish a reputation based on good advice, quality conversation and trust with the people you interact with, then when you do offer a link to a product that you like so much that you are affiliated with the company, people will know that it is a good choice and not care that you are getting a cut of the price. I've seen it work many times. But building that level of trust takes time, energy and commitment – that's why it's an advanced use.

Facebook and other niche social media websites allow developers to produce games and other engaging software to allow interaction between users. Many of these applications are monetized with affiliate offers. There are two main ways that they drive traffic. One is through simple banner adverts. The other is that they make the user earn points to use the application. In order to get points the user has to complete an affiliate offer, which could be to buy an affiliate merchant's product. For example, Farmville is a game loved by millions on Facebook. In order to grow your farm you need to collect points. You can get points by completing affiliate offers (like a request form for a new toothpaste sample). There has been some criticism of this because people only complete the offers to grow their farms, not because they are interested in the products.

Some of this traffic has been criticized for being of low quality. However, with the growth of social media and its penetration of different social demographics, I believe it is a young but growing field in affiliate marketing.

 WHAT THE FUTURE HOLDS

Affiliate marketing will only continue to evolve as the Internet itself becomes more sophisticated and streamlined. I see two areas that could explode as they integrate with affiliate marketing strategies.

MOBILE AND LOCATION-BASED AFFILIATES

Businesses are already rushing to create their own apps on mobile devices, and location-based services like Foursquare and Gowalla are gaining members consistently. A few early-adopter businesses have begun offering deals through mobile, location-based services, and I'm waiting for everyone to catch on. This could be a big market for local affiliates, who would know a city or neighborhood well and become the middle-people for positioning and managing deals on those networks. Connecting businesses with group offers that are in line with local festivals or holidays or simply things that are happening on a given day could become a lucrative market, especially if combined with the rise of group purchasing, which I also think is in the future of affiliate marketing.

GROUP PURCHASING

There are services that utilize group purchasing power to obtain large discounts. An example is Groupon in the United States. Groupon has a huge email list of subscribers and each day they send out a link to a local deal at a particular establishment. They need a certain number of people to say that they will buy the deal, and when they do, everyone who has signed up for that day's deal automatically buys the deal. To participate, a business registers a deal with Groupon and says that they will offer a certain deal if a certain number of people buy it. For example, a restaurant may offer a 2-for-1 dinner coupon if 50 people buy it. Groupon then sets a date and sends out the deal to their email list.

"Affiliate Marketing has been an excellent channel for many smaller and start-up ecommerce sites. Unlike the large big name brands, which are overrun with adware and toolbars, the little guys get the content sites which add value and send them new customers. They usually realize which coupon sites are good and bad by removing the ones who only send traffic by showing up for their domain + coupons (yourURL. com coupon code) in Google or other search engines. They are also usually the first to react when they find out about adware, which their outsourced program managers and the Networks usually deny exists. They keep an open and fair playing field which is why I see them as the most successful and largest growing legit Affiliate Marketing group. The nice thing for them is that with content only sites in their program, it is pure value add and no risk for them. I see more small merchants moving back into the affiliate space in the future and I see a lot of the larger brands starting to pull back out, mainly because of the new FTC tax laws and as they discover the toolbar and adware theft the Networks have hidden from them for so long. As far as the future of Affiliate promotions, I have been seeing both Share a Sale (my preferred network) and Linkshare links going through my iPhone. I have also seen my clients mobile sales on a steady increase quarter over quarter and it becoming a solid and reliable revenue stream. Affiliates are usually the first into these spaces because of the lack of red tape and the large amount of creativity and drive they have. I can easily see them driving the way into more successful shopping apps, streaming out deals to smartphones for shopping and further incorporating online to off-line sales via mobile and social media with full tracking capability. Call to conversion is already in place, so picking up and recording the tracking in a store can be an easy next step. Mobile, Social and Online to Off-line are definitely quickly growing and very profitable next moves in the future of Affiliate Marketing."

Adam Riemer

Adam Riemer is the president of Adam Riemer Marketing, LLC (www.adamriemer.me). He has been in online marketing for over a decade and helped companies from mom and pop shops to the Fortune 500 with everything from Datafeed and Affiliate Marketing to Social Media and Sales Funneling. His passion for ethical and adware free marketing has enabled him to help companies grow, increase their bottom line by removing theft and got him invitations to speak at various shows including Affiliate Summit, Pubcon and USPS Social Media Summit.

> "There is a lot of opportunity for affiliates and merchants both in the coming years as a sales and income channel. Mobile is up and coming, plus I see a lot of growth in the B2B (business to business) area. With the current economy many people need to supplement their income from their day job or have lost their jobs completely and need to make money somehow. Some of these entrepreneurs become affiliates and others start companies to sell products or services. eCommerce overall has no where to go but up."
>
> Deborah Carney

Deborah Carney started as an affiliate marketer over 15 years ago, back at the beginning with Amazon and Commission Junction. She has been an affiliate manager and consultant for over 5 years and has podcasts to help affiliates, bloggers and merchants grow their businesses. MerchantABCS.com is where you can find training for merchants considering starting affiliate programs that Deborah has developed. There is an overview of affiliate marketing and if merchants decide that affiliate marketing is for them there is additional training on how to start and manage their programs. Deborah is the administrator of two forums about affiliate marketing, ABCsPlus.com and AffiliateSummit.com/forum

t TOOLS AND RESOURCES

1   **Affiliate Summit** (www.affiliatesummit.com). Affiliate Summit is a conference that brings together agencies, affiliates, merchants, networks, and vendors and provides educational sessions on industry issues and fosters a productive networking environment for affiliate marketers. They hold several major summits across the United States each year.

2   **MurrayNewlands.com** (www.murraynewlands.com). My blog offers a lot of useful information about the affiliate marketing world!

3   **Affiliate forums.** There are lots of great affiliate forums: www.abestweb.com; www.abcsplus.com; www.affiliates4u.com.

4   **VigLink** (www.Viglink.com). This service enables website owners to add a simple code (a few javascript lines) to their sites to add affiliate links to all their pages.

5   **Azam Marketing** (www.azam.net). Having been at the vanguard of affiliate marketing since 1997, Azam Marketing provides a variety of services to get you up and running.

Chapter 10

Digital Advertising

INTRODUCTION

Some people say that advertising is the second oldest profession in the world. While that may be up for debate, it's true that advertising must have begun around the time that one person had the same product or service as someone else – and wanted to get the word out that what they were offering was better. In this time of the evolving Internet, though, advertising is changing at a rapid pace.

The basics are still the same: you want to bring your product or service to the attention of customers. You still make a plan based on your goals, identify target markets, create relevant messaging, place ads where your customers are, and then implement your ads as part of a larger media plan. What is different is the options for where you put those ads, what you can do to help them be successful, and how you determine their effectiveness.

The key things you'll need to think about for any ad campaign are contextualization, relevancy, consumer acceptance, and how all of these different options fit in with your campaign goals. Why? One of the big things that *has* changed about advertising is how much control people have over what they see. People determine what kind of advertising they view in the online space – whether that is through the search terms they are looking for, their profile information on a social network or their choice of which websites to visit. It means that you need to be strategic about where you place your ads, and that consumer reaction to them is more important than it was in the time of traditional broadcast advertising.

This chapter will focus on four advertising platforms that I believe are the most widespread and effective in the online and social media space. I will cover:

1 Google Adwords
2 Facebook Ads
3 Promoted Tweets
4 Banner ads

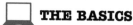 **THE BASICS**

Advertising has not gone away, it's just changing. Millions of dollars are spent every year in the online advertising space, and consumers increasingly have more of a voice about which ads they see. With Adwords, people determine the ads they see by what they search for. With Facebook, it's their profile information. On Twitter, Promoted Tweets only stay on the page as long as they are getting enough ReTweets from the people who are active on Twitter. And with banners, consumers will see the ads that are on the sites they visit – and that's their decision.

1 ADWORDS

Adwords is one of the most globally embraced forums of online advertising, and with good reason. There are billions of queries on Google's search engine every year, and that is the ideal time to get your name in front of customers – when they are looking for a product or service that you provide.

When you go to Google.com and type in a search term, Google uses a complex algorithm to return what it thinks are the most relevant links, images and other search suggestions based on the words you type in. On your search results page, the results take up the middle of the screen. On the right side of the page, and sometimes at the very top of the list of search results, there are a variety of Sponsored Links – these Sponsored Links are there because those companies paid for them to be there through Adwords.

When you sign up for Adwords, you write your own basic ad, choose the search terms (keywords) you want your ad to appear for, and decide how much money you want to spend per click and your per day maximum. One of the reasons Adwords is so popular is that they only charge you when someone clicks on your ad, not every time it appears on the page.

How far up the list of Sponsored Links your link appears is based on a combination of how much you are willing to pay per click and how relevant your ad's keywords are to the word(s) the Google searcher typed in. I'll say more on the ad structure and the bidding competitions it creates later.

Developing campaign strategies to meet business objectives is an art form. From selecting keywords and writing advertising copy along with bid price and optimizing the campaign is a ongoing talk, done well it can generate sales overnight, done badly you can waste money fast.

There are other pay-per-click platforms, but Adwords is clearly the most utilized because of Google's ubiquity as a search engine. If you have success with a Google adwords campaign, you can take that success and duplicate it on other lesser-known but less expensive pay-per-click platforms.

2   FACEBOOK ADS

With well over a half a billion users, Facebook is the one of the largest online social networks there is. And luckily for us, they have made it an advertiser-friendly space. The basics for Facebook advertising are similar to Google Adwords, but you can also determine not only what a user is looking at and you can focus more on what people are interested in. There is more demographic targeting based on their preferences.

Facebook Ads are displayed on the right side of a user's profile page, and what ads display are based on the information contained in the user's profile. The targeting can get extremely specific, as you are able to filter who sees your ad by geography, age, gender, education, relationship status, workplace and keywords.

Similarly to Google Adwords, you then select keywords and decide how much you want to spend per word and per day. With Facebook Ads you also have the option to either pay based on cost per click (CPC) or cost per thousand page views (CPM).

The key differences from Facebook Ads compared to Google Ads is that the more targeted you are with your Facebook Ads the less money it costs you.

3   PROMOTED TWEETS

Twitter spent a couple of years offering a free service that grew exponentially but had no model for making money – and they took a lot of flak from people in the business world for not having a business plan that would make them money. Meanwhile they raised millions of dollars in venture capital. In the summer of 2010 they launched "Promoted Tweets." What is a Promoted Tweet? Twitter themselves defined it this way on their blog: "Promoted Tweets are ordinary Tweets that businesses and organizations want to highlight to a wider group of users."

On the right side of a Twitter page is a list of the Top Ten Trending topics at that time. A business or organization can pay Twitter to include their Promoted Tweet at the bottom of that list. When users click on that link, they are taken to a Twitter search page for that term, where the Promoted Tweet is at the top of the page and above the real-time feed.

Twitter makes a big deal out of the fact that these Promoted Tweets begin as organic parts of the Twitter stream from that company, and that if the tweets do not "resonate" with users – meaning they don't get Replies and/or ReTweets – they will disappear from the stream.

4   DIFFERENT TYPES OF BANNERS

Advertising banners were one of the first kinds of advertising on the Internet, and they bear the closest resemblance to traditional advertising like billboards, print ads, or even television ads. You see them everywhere – and you probably know most of the tricks by now. Some are flashy, some include animations, and some try to pose as anything but an ad. If you are going to buy banner advertising space on websites, I recommend that you buy it on targeted websites that are writing about what you are selling, and I recommend that you stay away from trickery in your ad. People are discerning and the last thing you want is a bad name for your company in the advertising world.

The two biggest recent innovations in banner ads are that they now include robust data collection forms (banners used to be just graphics: now whole survey forms can be included in banners), and the customization of the ad sizes across different websites.

HOW TO USE IT IN PRACTICE

1   ADWORDS

When someone does a search on Google, they are searching for specific topics and websites that relate to the words in their search. Google adverts places ads according to the words a user types into the Google search engine. As an advertiser using Adwords, your basic goal is to choose keywords that match the words your potential customers type into the search box, though of course, it's a little more complicated than just that.

Starting out

Your first step is opening a Google Account and registering for Adwords at: www.adwords.google.com/um/Signup. To start, you'll need to specify what country and time zone you are in, as well as what currency you will be paying with. From there, Google has a great walk-through that will show you how to set up your account and start creating ads.

- **Keyword tool.** The Google Keyword Tool is a critical component of your research and planning. On this page you can type in keywords that you are considering targeting your ads with, and Google will tell you the global and local search volumes so that you know how many people are searching for those terms.

   If you are just starting out with an Adwords campaign, I recommend starting with a reasonable monthly budget that is part of your existing ad spend. For the most part, the higher the search volume, the higher the cost of getting your ad on the page will be. For this reason, you should spend the first few months trying out terms that have lower search volumes where you know your ad will get on the page.

   Doing research with the keyword tool will allow you to find a broader range of keywords that are relevant to your product or service. It is possible to advertise against broader search terms (e.g. scissors), as well as niche terms (e.g. red, left-handed scissors).

- **Cost.** The big difference between Google Adwords and traditional banner ad campaigns is that it is priced on a cost-per-click (CPC) rather than a cost-per-impression basis. It is therefore viewed as more targeted and more related to performance than per-impression (per-impression means every time the advert is displayed on the screen to a user) advertising. You only pay when someone clicks on the advertisement, which means that you only pay when someone is interested and sees your ad as relevant content.

  It's set up in such a way that you can start with a very small budget and choose how much money you spend on a daily or click performance basis.

- **Google Auction and Your Quality Score.** How much you pay is determined by what you are willing to spend and the users' actual interest in the advert that you are offering. The higher the propensity of the users to click on the advertisements, the lower the cost that you will have to spend.

  Every time a user types in a Google search, Google runs an "auction" within their Adwords software to determine which advertisements appear and what order they appear in. When you sign up for Google Adwords you have to put in a maximum bid for each of your keywords. When a user does a search for that keyword, Google selects the top bids for that keyword and displays them in descending order.

  But it's not quite that simple. They also rank your ad according to something they call your Quality Score, which is based on an internal Google formula that consists of three parts: your Click Thru Rate (CTR), the Relevance of your ad to the search query, and your Landing Page's quality.

To determine the actual placement of your ad, Google multiplies your bid times your Quality Score to create your "Ad Rank." It then displays the ads based on which ad has the highest ad rank.

Your cost is the minimum amount that keeps your ad in that position after Google has done the calculation. For that reason, your cost changes every time your ad is displayed if someone clicks on it, and that's why Google asks for a maximum spend per day.

- **Tracking.** It is possible to put some more tracking software on your own website, which allows you to optimize your advertising against more specific search terms that give you the best return on investment. One example of this is the kind of software that will display different adverts from different companies and display the advert which has the biggest number of clicks per 100 users.

2 FACEBOOK

Just like Google Ads, Facebook Ads are displayed on the right side of the page. But Facebook Ads go beyond Google Ads in that they are customized not only to the behavior of the user but to the profile information that users have entered.

Facebook advertising is powerful because of how targeted it can be. Ads can be targeted at very specific groups through things like geography, age, gender and workplace – even relationship status. Your challenge is to choose a keyword that hits the sweet spot – one that reaches enough people but not too many, and that will take some trial and error on your part.

In any Facebook Ad, you get 25 characters in your headline, 135 for the body text, and can upload one picture. This picture is critical, as it is what makes your ad pop out on the side of the page. You have the option of purchasing a cost-per-click (CPC) model or a cost-per-thousand (CPM) model where you pay per 1000 ad views. Regardless of which one you choose, you'll have to put in an initial bid. Facebook recommends starting at around $50 or £35, and that's a good place to start.

The key thing about creating Facebook Ads is to test your ads for effectiveness. Because the photo is so critical to the success of your ad, I recommend creating three or four versions of the same ad with different pictures. After testing it for a day or two, refer to the Facebook Insights tool to see what's working and what isn't. Keep the ad or ads with the highest number of clicks, or try other versions.

You can link your Facebook Ad to something external (like your own website or a sales page), but if you are using the ad to promote something within Facebook, there are a few things to keep in mind. If you use the ad to promote an event, keep in mind that your ad will automatically use the title of your event in the ad. In addition, Facebook will automatically add "RSVP to this event." Additionally, if you place an ad for your Facebook page, "Become a fan" is automatically part of the ad.

3   PROMOTED TWEETS

At the time of writing this book, Promoted Tweets was still in the testing phase, but I decided to include it because I believe it will be an important player in online advertising for a long time to come. I can't go into detail about how it works since I have only seen them work with test companies, but I speculate that the basic structure of a Promoted Tweet will be this:

Your company creates a regular tweet that goes out into your Twitter stream. You then go to a registration page of some sort within the Twitter website where you identify that tweet as something you want to promote. Twitter will then display that tweet at the top of searches for the keywords you select.

4 BANNER ADS

To create a banner advertising campaign, you need the banner adverts you want to use in a .gif or. jpg format (known as creative) and money. Whereas Adwords, Facebook Ads and Promoted Tweets create the actual visual for you based on what you type in, banner ads will require you or a graphic designer that you hire to create the advertisement.

Once you have your banner ad created, you'll need to pay a website based on the number of page views that they get on average. The standard in this field is that you would pay a set cost-per-thousand (CPM) clicks, where M is the Roman numeral for thousand.

 **EXAMPLES**

1 GOOGLE ADWORDS

If you use Google, you know how Google Adwords works. Rather than me giving you an example, go to Google and search for an obscure term and note what ads come up. Looking at Google Adwords contextual results with the eye of an advertiser or marketer is completely different than looking at it as an everyday searcher.

2 FACEBOOK ADVERTISING

Groupon: I spend a good amount of my time in San Francisco, and one of the advertisements on Facebook that is popular in there is for a collective purchasing discount company called Groupon. Their approach to Facebook advertising is simple – show a picture of a colorful cupcake, which most people want, and advertise "Up to 70% off on local deals." Both compelling and true.

3 PROMOTED TWEETS

Virgin America: The airline chose to announce their 2010 expansion into Canada only on Twitter using Promoted Tweets. The promotional offer included in the tweet gave 50% off to the first 500 travelers who bought tickets. They sold out in just three hours, and the day went on to become Virgin's fifth highest sales day in history.

4 BANNER ADS

YouTube leaderboard ads are some of the most interesting and compelling banner ads around right now. I won't pick one out as better than the others, but look to what is going on at the top of the YouTube homepage for an idea of where banner ads are going in the future.

ADVANCED USES

ADWORDS

Adwords is based on a somewhat complicated formula that recalculates with each search query. Advanced users are advertisers who are good at tracking the kind of results that come from the various bids they make on search terms. You can improve your results by finding new keywords to target. These can be based on a number of things, such as seasonal changes (i.e. Christmas shopping habits) and other campaigns going within the company.

FACEBOOK AND PROMOTED TWEETS: INTEGRATION

Because Facebook Ads and Promoted Tweets exist on social media networks, the easiest way to help your campaign succeed is to make sure it is part of a larger marketing push. Facebook Ads on their own will be limited in their reach, but integrating a targeted Facebook Ad campaign around launching a new product or service in a localized area will help raise the visibility of your launch significantly. The same goes for Promoted Tweets – they will only have so much impact on their own, but if you time them with a larger Twitter and social media push, they will hold their position because of the conversations and sharing that that campaign generates as well.

BANNER ADS: STANDING OUT, AND COUNTING

Banner Ads are everywhere. As one of the oldest forms of advertising on the Internet, they are still a big business, but because people have gotten so good at ignoring them or disciplining themselves to not click on them, they don't have nearly the power or returns that they used to have. You need to make your banner ads stand out, either by making them visually unique or by offering something of uncommon value. Some ads are already expanding over text when the user hovers their mouse on top, and ads are increasingly running videos – look for this kind of visual differentiation to get even more competitive and creative.

WHAT THE FUTURE HOLDS

1   INCREASINGLY TARGETED

Online advertising is increasingly moving toward more specific target-ing – the holy grail being providing a user with exactly what they are looking for when they do a search or log in to their social media net-work. This kind of targeted advertising will get more targeted as online information gathering improves, as well as the spread of location-based apps for smartphones. I see advertising taking a tip from marketing and starting to try to attract attention by offering something of value, not just being flashy.

2   MOBILE INTEGRATION

Smartphones are changing the way business is done on the Internet. With more and more websites creating apps to customize the user experience on those smartphones, look for the way that advertising is targeted through profile customization and search query relevance to break through to mobile. The potential for advertisers to give you what you want based on your past behavior and habits will happen.

3   RELEVANCE

Relevance is a key consideration for advertisers. Consumers now expect the advertising to be real, truthful and relevant. And at the same time, the government is getting involved – whether that means regulating the blogging industry for doing paid posting or looking at what Internet advertising does to users' computers around cookies and behavior tracking.

TOOLS AND RESOURCES

ADWORDS

- **Google Adwords Help** (www.adwords.google.com/support). They get a lot of questions about Adwords, believe me. They know how to answer them.
- **Perry Marshall** (www.perrymarshall.com). He's a blogger and coach who focuses specifically on how to do Adwords right – definitely worth the read.

FACEBOOK ADVERTISING

- **Facebook Advertising Term Glossary** (www.facebook.com/help/?page=859). This is a great library of term definitions so you can be sure you know what you're talking about.
- **Facebook Ad Tactics** (www.facebookadtactics.com). This is a great blog dedicated specifically to discussing everything new around Facebook advertising tactics – the articles are genuine and always helpful and thoughtful.

TWITTER

- **Twitter** (www.support.twitter.com/articles/142101-promoted-tweets-amp-promoted-trends). If you need help with Promoted Tweets, talk to Twitter.

Index